PROVERBS
ECCLESIASTES
John J. Collins

KNOX PREACHING GUIDES
John H. Hayes, Editor

John Knox Press
ATLANTA

Library of Congress Cataloging in Publication Data

Collins, John Joseph, 1946–
    Proverbs, Ecclesiastes.

    (Knox preaching guides)
    Bibliography: p.
    1. Bible. O.T. Ecclesiastes—Commentaries.
    3. Bible. O.T. Proverbs—Commentaries.
    3. Bible. O.T. Eclesiastaries—Homiletical use.
    4. Bible. O.T. Proverbs—Homiletical use.
    I. Title.
    II. Series.
    BS1475.3.C64   223'.707   79-92067
    ISBN 0-8042-3218-0

©copyright John Knox Press 1980
10 9 8 7 6 5 4 3 2 1
Printed in the United States of America
John Knox Press
Atlanta, Georgia 30365

CONTENTS

NOTE: The sections in Proverbs correspond to distinct collections which are indicated as such in the text. There are no such sections in Ecclesiastes.

ECCLESIASTES

Introduction

At the end of the book of Ecclesiastes we are told that "the Preacher also taught the people knowledge, weighing and studying and arranging proverbs with great care" (12:9). It is hardly necessary to say that no one today would formulate the job description of a preacher in quite that way. Proverbs are not "where it's at," in modern western society, and haven't been there for longer than anyone can remember. The crisis of relevance, which confronts any preacher who tries to bring to life a two-thousand year old scripture, is especially acute in books like Proverbs and Ecclesiastes. The prophets speak boldy against the abuse of power and wealth, a message which seems in no danger of losing its relevance. The story of the Exodus is repeatedly rediscovered as a paradigm for modern liberation movements. Even the bloodier tales of the conquest and the Judges, which are not always suitable for Sunday school, can be guaranteed to hold the interest of an adult audience. Proverbs, by contrast, do not readily provide inspiration or excitement. With the exception of Leviticus, it is doubtful that any biblical book is viewed with less enthusiasm by the preacher.

The present volume proceeds from the conviction that Proverbs and Ecclesiastes both deserve and can arouse far more enthusiasm than is usually accorded to them. The problem of relevance is at bottom the problem of integrating our own experience with the biblical text. No biblical books deal more directly than these with the kinds of human experience common to us all. These books illustrate how theological reflection can arise out of ordinary everyday human experience. Theology does not depend on miracles, or on exceptional events that happened long ago and in a far country, but can arise from the experiences of birth and death, joy and sorrow that are common to all. True, Proverbs and Ecclesiastes will not excite us with many new and surprising insights. Ecclesiastes maintains that there is nothing new under the sun. What they have to offer is not novelty, but depth. They invite us to reflect on what it means to be human, to be creatures of God. This is not a new problem, or one that electrifies the imagination of the day, but it is a fundamental problem, and one that will never go out of fashion or go away.

Despite the fact that they deal with "ordinary" human experiences, as opposed to extraordinary ones like the exodus, Proverbs and Ecclesiastes often seem more strange to the modern preacher than other biblical books. Most preachers are accustomed, from their theological education, to the rhetoric of "acts of God" and "thus says the Lord." The very lack of such "supernatural" language in Proverbs and Ecclesiastes makes them seem odd, and causes some people to wonder how they came to be part of the Bible. The fact that these books have become somewhat strange can itself be of some benefit to the preacher, since it offers the possibility of a fresh perspective, different from what we usually think of as biblical theology. However, if we are to benefit from the strangeness of these biblical books we must first come to understand the kind of literature to which they belong, and the way it fits in with the rest of scripture.

The Wisdom Literature

Proverbs and Ecclesiastes belong to the category "wisdom literature." This category is not confined to collections of proverbs (the only other such collection in the biblical corpus is the deutero-canonical book of Sirach or Ecclesiasticus). The OT wisdom literature includes the book of Job, which is partially a story but largely a dialogue, and which develops a single theme at great length throughout the book. It also includes the deutero-canonical Wisdom of Solomon, which contains few proverbs, but is rather a philosophical reflection on the nature of the world and the fate of the righteous. A few psalms (1, 32, 34, 37, 49, 112, 128) are usually classified as wisdom and some (but not all) scholars would extend the category to include stories such as Esther and the Joseph story in Genesis. It is obvious then that wisdom does not refer to a single literary form. Rather it refers to a set of presuppositions, or, if you prefer, to an approach to theology.

What Wisdom Is Not

As is often the case when we try to come to grips with a phenomenon such as wisdom, it is easier to say what it is not than what it is. Anyone who reads through the OT will be struck by what appear to be omissions in Proverbs and Ecclesiastes. To begin with, there is no talk of "salvation history" or even of the history of Israel at all. We find references to God, to be sure, but he is not said to "act" in the same dramatic way as in the exodus. The wisdom literature is not concerned with miracles, or indeed with the supernatural. Only in the later deutero-canonical wisdom books of Sirach and the Wisdom of Solomon do we find treatments of the history of Israel, and then we find theological reflections rather than the direct recitation of the story. In the early wisdom books of Proverbs and Ecclesiastes (and in Job, too) the specific experience of Israel is ignored. So too is the tradition of a God who spoke to his chosen people. The wise men never thunder "Thus says the Lord" or presume to speak in his name. Their God is silent, as Job's God is silent through the time of his suffering. The voice from the storm-cloud at the end of the book of Job is a dramatic exception which has no parallel in Proverbs and Ecclesiastes. The wisdom literature does not take its point of departure from any special revelation, or even from a clearly published divine law or covenant. Its root is neither at the Reed Sea nor at Sinai.

It would be a great mistake, however, to think of wisdom as a defective theology which lacks the fulness of divine revelation. The omissions are significant and they reflect an approach to theology which is fundamentally different from what we often assume to be "biblical theology." It is very easy (and, for preachers, very tempting) to read the Bible, and especially the OT, as it were, from God's point of view. Much of the OT has God as the subject who acts or speaks, and may give us the impression that we know what God did or said in a clear and unambiguous way. From this point of view the Bible is the record of a *Supernatural* Revelation. Utilizing such a view, biblical theology (and the biblically based preacher!) can speak with divine authority and expound the will of God with the clearcut confidence that it is definitively right. The idea that one has a divine, supernatural source of authority is understandably attractive for the preacher. Further, for Protestant preachers whose theological training was heavily influenced by Karl Barth and the Neo-orthodox movement, such an approach to the Bible may be almost inevitable. This is not the place to argue the inadequacy of such an approach to the

Bible as a whole. What concerns us here is the wisdom literature, and it is quite obvious that proverbial wisdom raises
problems for any approach that regards the Bible as purely
supernatural revelation.

Wisdom as Natural Theology

By not building on either the prophetic claims of divine
inspiration or the traditional claims of divine revelation in the
history of Israel, the wisdom books leave no doubt that their
approach is from the human point of view, not God's. *Wisdom
theology is natural theology, not supernatural.* The phrase "natural theology" may call for some clarification since it has often been used in the history of Christian theology to refer to
many different things. I use the phrase here deliberately in
contrast to "supernatural" to indicate the starting point of
theology: in natural theology, we do not have at our disposal a
definitive divine revelation, but we have to build our own theology by accumulating and interpreting our human experience of life, nature and the world. Given that starting-point,
different people can reach very different conclusions. There
have been "natural theologies" based on different philosophical systems (e.g. Thomism, Process philosophy) which are as
different in their theology as in their underlying philosophy.
When I say that wisdom theology is natural theology I am not
saying that it should be tied to any particular philosophy, but
that it should be understood as a philosophy in itself, as an attempt to make sense of human experience, from the human
point of view. Just what sort of philosophy is found in Proverbs and Ecclesiastes will become apparent as we go through
the commentary.

One other comment on "natural theology" is perhaps in
order. It would be a great mistake to think of natural theology
as an arrogant assertion that humanity can solve all its own
problems and does not need divine revelation. It can of course
be used that way—theologians and preachers are as prone to
arrogance as the rest of humanity. In principle, however, natural theology is rather more modest than its "supernatural"
counterpart. A theology which claims to be based on a definitive divine revelation may try to give all the credit to God, but
in practice can hardly avoid feeling smug that it knows all the

answers. A self-consciously human or natural theology, by contrast, has no divinely guaranteed answers and so is constantly reminded of its human limitations.

Practical Implications

The difference between the type of natural theology which we find in the wisdom literature and the "supernatural" approach to biblical theology is of immense practical significance for the preacher. The significance is not a matter of specific ideas or doctrines but rather of an entire approach to preaching and to theology. The task of the preacher, from the perspective of wisdom, is not to expound doctrines, or even to repeat the story of "salvation history." It is to probe human experience and try to make sense of it. The test of preaching is not whether it conforms to preconceived, revealed doctrines, but the adequacy with which it explains human experience. The wisdom books do not offer the preacher any ready guarantee of divine authority, but they invite him or her to derive authority from experience, and to give full weight to that experience in dealing with theological and moral questions. The experience of the preacher and the audience is not merely material for illustrating biblical and church doctrine. It can be the very stuff of theology, and is at once the greatest resource for the preacher.

In the light of these remarks it should be obvious that our purpose in commenting on Proverbs and Ecclesiastes can not be to extract ideas or doctrines from these books. We will try to see the kinds of questions raised in these books and the ways in which they are answered. The particular solutions they propose (if one can indeed say that a book like Ecclesiastes proposes solutions at all!) will not always address our problems, but we can at least learn from their way of approach.

The Role of Experience

Biblical scholarship has long learned to be wary of deriving easy answers and simplistic solutions for modern questions and problems from the Bible. The reason is, of course, that the experience of the biblical writers was conditioned by their time and place and may be very different from ours. This consideration raises a particular problem for the type of theology which we find in the wisdom books. We have said that wisdom theology is based on human experience. But, someone may ask, whose experience? Is not human experience notoriously diversified? Can we then accord any authority to the experience of scribes or peasants in the ancient Near East, when our experience is that of the technological, urbanized, modern West?

Any theology based on experience must ultimately answer the question "whose experience?" with "our own." The point is made forcefully in the book of Job. The friends of Job can muster an impressive set of arguments drawn from the tradition, all of which were undoubtedly supported by somebody's experience. Job, however, was unimpressed. The experience of his forefathers could not take precedence over his own. At the end of the book, Job is commended for his honesty. The point is not that Job was right—in fact he is put down rather severely by the voice from the stormcloud. The experience of any individual is limited and fallible. But in the last analysis our own experience is our final yardstick by which we have to measure what others tell us. No responsible adult can lightly throw that yardstick aside.

The importance of the experience of the individual will be clearly evident in Ecclesiastes. Even there, of course, we are by no means dealing with autobiography. The sages could always draw on the accumulated wisdom of the tradition to fill out their own experience and give it perspective. Proverbs 10– 29 is quite clearly a collection of traditional sayings. The sayings repeatedly urge respect for tradition. "Listen, my son, to your father's teaching" is as typical of wisdom as "thus says the Lord" is of prophecy. The wise man is always aware of his own limitations and willing to learn from others. However, the teaching of the father acquires its authority precisely from experience. The son should accept it because it accurately reflects what he will meet in life. Ultimately it will be tested by how well it fits the experience of the son. It does not claim a divine authority in and of itself.

The Common Human Experience

The experience of the individual has, then, a pivotal role in the wisdom literature. This does not mean that the wisdom books are preoccupied with experiences of a private and particular sort. On the contrary, it is typical of these books that they try to articulate what we might call common human experience—that is, the kind of experience which is potentially accessible to everyone by virtue of being human. We have said above that human experience is notoriously diverse, and this is true. Yet there are certain experiences and sentiments that are common to all—birth and death, love and hate, joy and sorrow, justice and injustice, wealth and poverty (although each of these can come in many forms). It is because of this common core that we can read and enjoy the literature of other races and ages, that Homer's epics or the story of Gilgamesh can still move us, and that the folklore of all races seems to return inevitably to very similar themes. This common core of apparently universal human experiences is the main concern of the sages, because they are not concerned with people as Jews or Gentiles or as any special class, but simply as human beings.

The Universalism of Wisdom

Here again we note the significance of the "omissions" we mentioned earlier. Proverbial wisdom pays no attention to the specific traditions of Israel. "Yahweh," the name of the god of Israel, is used for God, but most of what is written in Proverbs and Ecclesiastes could have been written by an Egyptian or Mesopotamian sage. Hebrew wisdom was part of a tradition of Near Eastern wisdom that can be traced back to the middle of the third millennium B.C., or about two thousand years before the book of Proverbs was written down. There is no doubt that biblical wisdom was influenced by its "pagan" predecessors, especially by Egyptian wisdom. (One section of Proverbs, 22:17 – 24:22, seems to depend directly on the Egyptian book of Amen-em-opet.) This international character is a very important aspect of proverbial wisdom. The fact that the sages could speak of their God in such an international idiom was a confident affirmation that their God was not the God of Israel alone, but of all humanity, and was in principle accessible to all. The significance of this attitude for the modern preacher should not be missed. Any preacher can choose to address his or her audience in "the language of faith," which specifically presupposes Christian beliefs and the context of the Church. Alternatively, he or she can adopt a broader horizon, speak the language of humanity at large and address problems that are not particularly Church problems but concern the wider society or the human condition. It is evident that any preaching informed by biblical wisdom cannot restrict itself to the inner-church context, but must take the wider view.

From this perspective issues such as poverty, urban decay or the decline in public education may be just as appropriate sermon topics as the doctrine of the Trinity or salvation by faith. It also means that a preacher who speaks on poverty or public education does not have to produce a distinctively Christian position on these issues. The question is not "what is the Christian thing to do?" but "what is the best and most practical thing to do?" Such problems as poverty and public education are equally obvious whether one is a believing Christian or not.

The fact that Proverbs and Ecclesiastes speak to and from common human experience means that their fundamental question is not what it means to be a believer (Jew or Christian) but what it means to be human. This point too is important for the preacher. True, there is no reason why a Christian preacher should not reflect on what it means to be a Christian, but we must beware of the narcissism of a faith that becomes preoccupied with the supposedly special status of a particular community. The wisdom tradition acknowledges no special status for any community. For wisdom, as for Paul, it matters little whether one is Jew or Greek. Wisdom and righteousness do not observe territorial or community boundaries.

Beyond Class Interest

Not all the sayings in Proverbs and Ecclesiastes are concerned with the universal aspects of human experience. Many sayings and the attitudes they express are undoubtedly shaped by the particular environment of the ancient Near East. The proverb that says "fear the Lord and the king" (Prov 24:21) certainly presupposes a society where there was a king and probably one where the king's power could not be effectively challenged anyway. In general, proverbial wisdom is cautious and resigned in its attitude and has sometimes been thought to reflect the viewpoint of a special and influential scribal class. It would be surprising indeed if the scribes who put these books together did not leave some trace of their particular attitudes. However, I think it would be a mistake to regard these books as the documents of one social class in any narrow sense. They are certainly not restricted to those problems which were peculiar to scribes. Ecclesiastes may be taken as the reflections of an individual scribe, but the origin of much of the material in Proverbs is quite uncertain. One section of Proverbs is introduced as "proverbs of Solomon which the men of Hezekiah king of Judah copied" (25:1). Now it is generally agreed that none of these proverbs can be assumed to come from Solomon himself, but we may take it that the men of Hezekiah (about 700 B.C.) made a collection of traditional proverbs. Not all of these were necessarily composed by scribes—they may have circulated anonymously "in the mouth of the people" as is often the case with proverbial lore. Subsequently, too, even those composed by scribes could be used by the common people in various situations. More importantly, as we shall see in the commentary, the perspective which dominates this literature is not determined by considerations which are peculiar to any class, but rather by those universal considerations which define what is common in human experience.

The books of Proverbs and Ecclesiastes are shaped, then, by the typical and recurring aspects of life rather than by particular and exceptional situations. For that reason we will not spend much time on the usual introductory questions of the date and place where these books were written. In the case of other biblical writings—for example the prophetic or apocalyptic books—it is very important to know what situation was involved. The prophets spoke to very specific crises and their advice would naturally vary according to the situation. Wisdom, by contrast, is the common, everyday fare which speaks to normal and typical situations. In fact there is general agreement that Proverbs 10–31 dates from the time before the exile. Most scholars date Proverbs 1–9 after the exile, but there is no clear evidence. The date of Ecclesiastes is widely disputed. Conjectures range from the seventh to the second century B.C., with perhaps a majority in favor of the fourth or third centuries. (Some would argue that the book was influenced by Greek philosophy, but the evidence is not conclusive.) The most significant point about the disputed dating is precisely the lack of clear evidence. This literature is not designed for specific unusual crises, but speaks to the common and typical aspects of life. Date and provenance contribute little to the understanding of this kind of literature.

The Relevance of a Wisdom Approach

Thus far we have tried to indicate the nature of wisdom as natural theology which seeks to understand common human experience. We have also noted that these books suggest an approach to theology and to preaching which concentrates on the experience of preacher and audience rather than on the proclamation of biblical or church doctrine. It is, I think, true to say that the time is ripe for such an emphasis and that many Christian audiences, who find traditional doctrines stale and uninspiring, are eager for an experiential approach. The so-called "secular" theology of the 1960's may have faded from the limelight, but it represented a widespread disillusionment with "supernatural" theology. That disillusionment was not a passing phenomenon but is deeply rooted in the modern mentality. It is also probably true that many preachers instinctively draw on the familiar experience of their audience rather than proclaim the tradition. Such preachers would do well to turn their attention to the wisdom literature, since it provides an example within the canon of a theology based uncompromisingly on human experience, without appeal to special revelation.

Some, however, may still have doubts about the legitimacy of such an approach. The wisdom literature is only a small portion of the biblical canon, and, some would say, peripheral. People who were taught in seminary to distinguish "a canon within the canon" may well be inclined to dismiss the wisdom books and feel that it is the duty of the preacher to proclaim the words and mighty deeds of the God of Israel. A full response to such an objection would require a detailed discussion of the nature of biblical theology. Without pretending to deal adequately with the subject we offer two considerations here.

Jesus and Wisdom

First, a factor that should carry some weight with any Christian preacher is that the preaching of Jesus, in so far as we can recover it, was to a very large degree wisdom preaching, based on the principles of what we have called "natural theology." The question as to how much of what is attributed to Jesus in the gospels was actually spoken by him, is of course, a very complicated one which we cannot take up here. There is general agreement however that the parables are the most distinctive form of his preaching. Parables are a wisdom form (although different from the shorter sayings of Proverbs and Ecclesiastes) in the sense that they are not presented as divine revelations and do not talk about the supernatural but tell a story in human terms which are in principle accessible to anyone. A single example will have to suffice. The story of the good Samaritan in Luke 10 tells how "a certain man" going from Jerusalem to Jericho is robbed and beaten. A priest and levite pass him by, but the unlikely Samaritan stops and takes care of him. The story, as Luke preserves it, ends with a question: "which of these three proved neighbor to the man who fell among the robbers?" The story is many-faceted, but two aspects of it particularly interest us here. First, the story concerns "a certain man." He is not identified as Jew or Gentile. All that the passersby can presumably see is a rather battered specimen of humanity but as such he represents Everyman and is the test of how we treat our fellow humans. The point here, that any human is every human, is a familiar NT theme and is in a sense the cutting edge of the doctrine of the incarnation. (Compare Matt 25:40: "as you did it to one of the least of these my brethren, you did it to me.")

The second point concerns the authority of the story. Everyone can see the answer to the question at the end: obviously the Samaritan did what was right. But the reason we know this is not because it was written in the Law or otherwise revealed. It didn't have to be revealed. We have only to imagine ourselves as the victim on the roadside to know what the situation demanded. The appeal of the story is not to our knowledge of revelation but to human commonsense. The message concerns not only what it means to be religious, but what it means to be human. The down-to-earth, human images of the teaching of Jesus stand in the tradition of wisdom in so far as their ultimate court of appeal is human experience.

The Prophets and Wisdom

Second, the wisdom literature is not nearly so peripheral to the OT as we might think. Many scholars in recent years have noted points of similarity between the prophetic and wisdom books (H. W. Wolff, *Amos the Prophet* [Philadelphia: Fortress, 1973] is an example). What concerns us here is not the use of proverbs or other literary forms by the prophets, but the cases of "wisdom-thinking" or natural theology. Two examples from Amos may suffice. In Amos 2:1 – 3 Moab is condemned "because he burned to lime the bones of the king of Edom." Now even if the act in question is in violation of some biblical law, the king of Moab could hardly be expected to know that. He could however be expected to know that what he did was a sin against humanity. His guilt is not that he broke the revealed law of God, but that he violated a natural human right. Again in Amos 9:7 Yahweh asks "Are you not like the Ethiopians to me, O people of Israel? Did I not bring up Israel from the land of Egypt, and the Philistines from Caphtor and the Syrians from Kir?" The point, that Israel is no more special in the eyes of God than Ethiopia, comes as a shock on the lips of a biblical prophet, and it is devastating for the traditional concept of a chosen people. Israel is, indeed, chosen (and the Church is too) but so is every other community in some way. God is not only the God of Jews or Christians, but of all humanity. This point too is typical of wisdom. Our common humanity is deeper and more significant than the distinctions of race or creed.

I am not suggesting that a prophet like Amos was influenced by a wisdom movement in some form. He did not have to be. Wisdom, after all, is primarily the attempt to base one's theology on common human experience. In so far as a prophet like Amos reflected on the nature of common humanity, he was in effect engaged in wisdom thinking. Wisdom is not simply a separate compartment away to the side of the OT. Wisdom thinking, as reflection on human experience, is rather a substratum of all religious thinking which can crop up in any context. As Lavinia, in Shaw's *Androcles and the Lion*, remarked: "I am not always a Christian. I don't think anybody is. There are moments when I forget all about it, and something comes out quite naturally." That which "comes out quite naturally" is wisdom. No one, not even a prophet, could go on forever reciting the mighty deeds of Yahweh. (Hopefully no preacher could either!) Sooner or later we inevitably fall back on the human knowledge gleaned from experience.

The Proverbial Form

Within the broader category of wisdom, Proverbs and Ecclesiastes are further distinguished by the fact that they are to a great extent collections of proverbs. Most of our introduction has dealt with the nature of wisdom. A few brief comments on the nature of proverbs may serve to conclude it. First, proverbs pose an obvious problem for preacher and commentator alike. To read straight through a few chapters of proverbs is like trying to have a conversation with someone who always replies with a one-liner. The first few may be amusing, but after a dozen or so it gets depressing! Need we say that proverbs are not designed for continuous reading, and in Prov 10– 31) is wasting his or her time? Proverbs are individual sayings which should be savored separately and in very small doses. In this commentary we will make no attempt to discuss every saying, or to say a little about everything. There are several excellent commentaries which provide verse by verse discussion. Rather we will try to illustrate how proverbs should be treated by taking a few significant examples from each unit.

One other point should be mentioned. Proverbs attempt to compress an insight into a short, striking sentence. Usually such compressed formulations are meant to be witty (and in fact they sometimes are!). Now if there is any one disease to which preachers and theologians are especially prone it is solemnity. A solemn reading or preaching of proverbs can be nothing less than catastrophic. It is of the essence of proverbs that they are true to a certain extent, but not absolutely, or that they fit some circumstances but not all. They are partial generalizations which apply to more than one case but not to all. So it is no surprise to find contradictory proverbs; the sage

who tells you that "he who hesitates is lost" will very probably also warn you to "look before you leap." Both pieces of advice are excellent, if you know when to apply them and when
to disregard them. (We will find a number of contradictory
sayings in the book of Proverbs: Prov 26:4–5 provides a famous example.) A solemn reading, which tries to take every
proverb seriously all the time, misses the whole point. Proverbs do not provide a handbook of hard factual information.
They are ambiguous and slippery and can expose the fool as
easily as they display the wise. As the sages warn us, a proverb
in the mouth of a fool is like a thorn that pierces the hand of a
drunkard (Prov 26:9). Let the preacher and commentator
beware!

PROVERBS

The Way of Wisdom and Life
(Proverbs 1 – 9)

The first nine chapters of Proverbs differ from the rest of the book in style and content. In style they are not simply collections of proverbs but several lengthy discourses. In content they are more theoretical and abstract than the rest of the book and are largely concerned with the personified figure of wisdom. We will reflect on what is meant by that figure as we go through the text.

The Call of Wisdom(1)

The Need for Understanding

The opening chapter sets the tone for the book. It falls into three sections—vv. 1 – 7, 8 – 19 and 20 – 33. The first of these is really a preface which sketches the program of the book. The objectives of the sage are worth some reflection. They are expressed by the repetition of a number of key words which are virtually synonymous—wisdom, knowledge, instruction, understanding. The matter to be understood includes righteousness and justice, but also proverbs and riddles—which need not be religious or edifying at all. The goal is "that prudence be given to the simple"—that people should have a realistic knowledge of the world they live in. We should note that there is no suggestion of idealism or of high principles which should be held through thick and thin. Still less is there any suggestion of what we might call blind faith. There have always been some circles in Christianity which hold an ideal of faith which is opposed to reason and understanding. Faith is thus conceived as an emotional matter of the heart, a warm glow in contrast to the cold light of reason. Sometimes faith has even been thought to demand a "sacrifice of the intellect" as if faith were purer when it is based on ignorance. The sages of Israel have no part in that sort of faith. Their comment is terse: those who despise wisdom and instruction are "fools" (1:7).

Yet the sages are no less devout for their respect for reason. Reason, they know, has its limits, and "the beginning of wisdom is the fear of the Lord" (1:7). The tone set by this phrase is one of respect and reverence, and this tone will be evident throughout the book. There is respect for the Lord whose wisdom surpasses all humanity; respect too for tradition, which leads the sages to ascribe all their lore to Solomon, the reputed fountainhead of the tradition. Finally there is respect for the superior experience of parents, which is constantly demanded (e.g. 1:8). The hardheaded knowledge of the scribes knows well the extent to which we depend on and are indebted to others. Respect for others (most obviously for God) and a humble attitude are the natural results of realistic self-knowledge. When a man is wise in his own eyes—and thus possesses no genuine humility—there is more hope for a fool than for him (26:12).

The Folly of Crime

Prov 1:8–19 is an extended warning not to go along with criminals who ambush innocent people to rob them. (Mugging is not a novelty of the modern city!). One observation may suffice here. We might expect a religious document to tell us that such conduct should be avoided because it is sinful, against the law of God and so forth. Not so Proverbs! The motivation is quite practical: violence leads to a violent death. In the long run, the criminal will lose out. Now a successful criminal might well dispute this, and no doubt there are exceptions, but it is typical of the logic of Proverbs. The preacher of Proverbs does not ask us to do anything because of an ideal, or an extrinsic law. Rather, what we should do is always ultimately in our own best interest. The ethics of wisdom are shaped to a great extent by the conviction that human beings depend on each other. The criminal, who violates the rights of other people, may one day find himself in need of them, and will have made enemies when he needs friends. The sages are, in general, cautious. It is safer to do to others as you want them to do to you. Some criminals may succeed, but is it worth the risk? This morality of Proverbs is not at all idealistic, but it is practical. It is built on the assumption that we can better persuade people to do what we think is good if we can show that it is ultimately in their own best interest.

Personified Wisdom

Prov 1:20 – 33 introduces the personified figure of wisdom. We usually think of wisdom as a quality or an attribute but not as a person. When we read "Wisdom cries aloud in the streets" we can readily see that this is a figure of speech, but what does it mean? We have at least a general idea of what wisdom stands for: it is an attitude to life, based on understanding. When we read that wisdom calls out to us, we are being told that it is not simply a human achievement. We do not simply acquire widsom by our own efforts (although we certainly do not acquire it without effort!). Wisdom is offered to us. The idea here is similar to the later Christian idea of grace. Wisdom is a gift.

By whom is this gift offered? In Prov 2:6, "the Lord gives wisdom," but in Prov 1 wisdom is said to offer itself. In fact, there is a very thin line between God and wisdom. Virtually everything that God is said to do in Proverbs can also be done by wisdom. Wisdom is the way in which God acts in the world. In the NT and in Christian theology much of what was said about wisdom in the OT is transferred to the Word (John 1) or to the Spirit, and so fully accepted as pertaining to the divine.

The personification of wisdom as we find it in Proverbs was historically a step towards the development of the doctrine of the Trinity. Its significance, however, is not merely historical. Like the whole idea of the Trinity, it suggests that there is more than one way of thinking and talking about the divine. In most of the OT and Christian theology God is conceived in strongly personal terms, and specifically in *mascu-*

line terms. He is Father or Son, Warrior or Shepherd. This usage is so deeply embedded in the tradition that we easily forget that these terms (even the masculine pronoun *he*) are only metaphors. It has been a merit of the feminist movement in recent years to have pointed out the limitation of our male-dominated God language. The wisdom tradition was aware of these limitations. Wisdom (a feminine noun in Hebrew) is personified as a woman. Even more basically, we are conscious that when we call wisdom a person we are speaking metaphorically. The same is true when we speak of God as a person. Now metaphors are important, and personality is surely appropriate when we talk about God, but we must remember that we do not encounter God in the same way that we encounter human persons. If God *calls* to us, it is in the same way that wisdom calls. We feel that something is attractive, and saying that God or wisdom calls is our attempt to explain why it is attractive.

We will see more of personified wisdom in the following chapters. We may feel that it is not as easy to relate to such an abstract figure as to the familiar traditional male image. However, the biblical tradition repeatedly warns us against identifying God with any image, graven or other. Any preacher must beware of the temptation to over-simplify God. At the very least, personified wisdom should serve to remind us that the divinity has many facets and should not be simply reduced to the dimensions of human personality.

These passages which speak of personified wisdom can be useful for the preacher in relating to the feminist problems with biblical God language. They can also provide a balancing corrective to some of the more crudely anthropomorphic notions of God in other biblical books. The divine warrior with blood on his garments (Isaiah 63) is not the only image of God that a biblically based preacher can offer to a modern audience.

Two other aspects of personified wisdom may be mentioned briefly for the present. First, where does wisdom cry out? Not from a pulpit! nor even in theological gatherings! but in the street and the market place. Religion, for the wisdom tradition, does not take us out of secular life but into the heart of it. Second, what does wisdom offer? The emphasis here is on security, freedom from fear, peace. The threat to the wicked is panic. The fruits of wisdom are developed at greater length in the following chapters.

The Fruits of Wisdom (2 – 4)

Chapters 2 – 4 present three collections of instructions. Each chapter is introduced by a sentence which calls on "my son" or "sons" to be attentive. We will not attempt to comment on every individual piece of advice, but will focus on the dominant themes.

The Two Ways

Throughout the three chapters we find a recurring contrast between two paths or ways: the path of wisdom and righteousness (2:7 – 9, 19 – 20; 3:6, 17, 23, 4:11, 18) and the path of folly and wickedness (2:12 – 15, 18; 4:14, 19). These paths are repeatedly characterized by polar opposites: e.g. life and death (2:18 – 19) or light and darkness (4:18 – 19). Before we proceed to look more closely at these two ways it may be well to ask whether it is good to preach in such clearly drawn contrasts. The book of Proverbs often leaves us with the impression that humanity is divided into two cleanly distinct categories, the righteous and the wicked, with no overlap and no ambiguity. Is this not a gross oversimplification of reality?

If we were to take these contrasts as absolute, they would indeed constitute a distortion of reality, and any preacher who uses clearcut distinctions of this sort should beware of the danger of oversimplification. However, it would be a mistake to take every formulation that we find in Proverbs as absolute truth; everything admits of some qualification. Even within these three chapters we find some caution: In 3:7 we read: "Be not wise in your own eyes." Even if you hold a clearcut distinction between the wise and the foolish, do not be too quick to assume that you are on the side of the wise! In fact, the kind of sharp contrasts we find in these chapters has little value as a description of humanity.

People can never be so cleanly divided between right and wrong. These contrasts must be seen quite simply as a teaching device. They construct two ideal types which are held up as models. They represent two tendencies or directions, between which the reader is urged to choose. The contrasts are deliberately overdrawn, so that the important features may

stand out more clearly. They are like caricatures or cartoons.
They do not attempt to show the nuances and shades, but to
make a basic point clearly. One might well say that effective
teaching and preaching always requires some oversimplification and especially clear contrasts. We never know what
something is unless we can say what it is not. It is the nature of
the human mind to think in contrasts and oppositions. The
clearcut contrast of the two ways can be useful, then, but we
must be quite clear on its limitations. It is a deliberately overdrawn caricature not an accurate description of reality.

Widsom is its Own Reward

The contrast between the two ways is made primarily in
terms of the consequences to which each leads. However, in a
peculiar manner, each way is itself its own reward or punishment. This point is immediately evident in Prov 2.

Chapter 2 is a direct exhortation to pursue wisdom, so
that certain positive results may be attained and negative
ones avoided. The main positive results are that "you will understand the fear of the Lord and find knowledge of God" (2:5)
and that "wisdom will come into your heart and knowledge
will be pleasant to your soul" (2:10). The reason to pursue wisdom, in short, is for its own sake, not for the sake of any by-
product or ulterior gain. Negatively, wisdom will deliver from
the way of evil, and from the "strange woman" (a figure who
seems to have fascinated the sages, and who will reappear in
the following chapters). Again, the avoidance of evil is its own
reward.

We have said at the beginning of this chapter that wisdom
is recommended because it is in the best interest of the reader
or listener. This idea may seem to clash with the view that
wisdom should be pursued for its own sake. We tend to think
that if wisdom is in our best interest we should *gain* something by it, acquire something, get something out of it over
and above wisdom itself. The desire for gain is not a modern
capitalist innovation. It is as old as humanity. Gain or profit,
however, is not the only thing that makes the quest of wisdom
worthwhile or in our interest. There is also the possibility of
enjoyment, in and of itself. Enjoyment, rather than gain, is the
goal of wisdom in both Proverbs and Ecclesiastes.

Material Rewards

It is of course true that ancient wisdom was often pursued for its profits, or, if you prefer, for its material rewards. In any case, even Proverbs and Ecclesiastes saw nothing wrong with material rewards—they do not preach a spiritual religion in any anti-material sense. Also, it is very difficult to express the advantages of enjoying wisdom without at least using the material rewards as analogies. The attitude of Proverbs to the rewards of wisdom becomes more fully evident in chapter 3.

The opening verses of Prov 3 promise the faithful son "length of days and years of life" and *shalom*, which we may translate as "general well-being." The two themes, life and well-being, are already present in chapter 2: the contrast between the way of life and the way of the strange woman in 2:18–19 and the promise that the upright will inhabit the land (2:21). The promise of material prosperity is most explicitly expressed in 3:9–10. If you honor Yahweh with your wealth, your barns and winevats will be filled. There is no doubt that material prosperity was often assumed to be a reward for virtue in antiquity, as we know, for example, from the book of Job, where the assumption is questioned. But is such an idea not utterly naive? or, worse, does it not simply reflect the complacency of the prosperous?

In general we should answer both these questions with "yes!" We should not be surprised that a canonical author shared to some extent the naiveté and complacency of his environment. The modern preacher should not presume that every statement in scripture is above reproach. The whole logic of the wisdom literature requires that we test these traditional claims in the light of experience. The book of Job was squarely within the wisdom tradition when it criticized the idea that prosperity or misfortune were signs of divine approval or punishment.

However, in fairness to the book of Proverbs we should point out that its final objective is not to guarantee full barns or winevats. These are at most signs and pointers, but the enjoyment of wisdom is something more. Prov 3:13–14 says explicitly that the "profit" (!) of wisdom is better than that of silver or gold, and that nothing we desire can compare with it. Why then does the author still speak of barns and vats and sil-

ver and gold? Because these are the best images we have for
the value of wisdom. A few points should be noted here. First,
wisdom is quite compatible with the appreciation of material
goods like wine and gold. Wisdom involves no asceticism and
it does not try to set "spiritual" values in opposition to material ones. Second, the value of wisdom can only be expressed
by images like these. Wisdom, after all, is understanding, and
it must always be the understanding of something in particular. Material goods can be objects of wisdom as well as any
other. There is no such thing as "pure" wisdom, independent
of any object. So wisdom can only be pursued through the understanding of the objects and experiences that make up this
world. Wisdom cannot be found in isolation from the world of
winevats and silver, but rather in the midst of that world (just
as wisdom in Prov 1 is said to find its forum in the streets and
market-places). The enjoyment of gold, or of wine, is not only
an analogy: it is a concrete instance of the enjoyment of wisdom, which shows what other instances are like.

The Theme of Life

The promised fruits of wisdom in 3:1 include not only the
well-being of *shalom* but also "length of days and years of
life." Again in 3:16 wisdom is said to have "long life in her
right hand" and riches in her left. Further, wisdom is "a tree
of life to those who lay hold of her" (3:18) and is "life" for the
soul (3:22). This theme is taken further in chapter 4 where we
read simply "she is your life" (4:13). The instruction in chapter 4 concludes with the admonition to "be attentive to my
words . . . for they are life to him who finds them and healing
to all his flesh" (4:22).

These few sentences indicate the range of what the sages
hoped for as "life." On the one hand, they quite frankly hoped
for "length of days" just they hoped for material prosperity.
The precepts of the sages might conceivably improve one's
chances of a long life because of their general caution and
avoidance of risks, but we must admit that it is naive to think
that wisdom automatically leads to a long life. On a second
level, however, life is used here metaphorically. Wisdom is a
tree of life, or even it *is* life. The first point that must be clearly
stated here is that the book of Proverbs does not envisage eternal life, and is not at all concerned with life after death. The

sages, like the ancient Israelites in general, believed in a shadowy afterlife in "Sheol," which was neither a heaven nor a hell but a neutral limbo. The hopes of the sages for the future were focused on "length of days" and on their progeny. However, when they say that wisdom is life, they are not thinking in terms of their future duration, but of the *quality of enjoyment* in the present. Throughout these chapters the sages search for ways to express the superlative value of wisdom: it is better than gold or silver, it is a way of light as opposed to darkness (4:18 – 19). The sages could scarcely say that wisdom is better than life, since it presupposes life: only the living can enjoy it. But the highest value they could place on wisdom is to say that it is the *fullness* of life. In effect, it is wisdom most of all that makes life worth living. The promise that wisdom gives life should not, then, be thought to suggest that wisdom is subservient to a final goal of gaining admission to immortality in another world. Here as always wisdom is thoroughly oriented to this life and this world, and the enjoyment of wisdom is itself life in the fullest sense.

At this point the Christian preacher may be tempted to add that the ideas of the sages have been superseded by Christian revelation on the afterlife. It is not possible here to discuss in detail the Christian idea of afterlife (or rather ideas, since there is variety even within the NT) and the use and abuse to which it can be subjected. It would be well, however, to remember that "eye hath not seen nor ear heard" what precisely happens after death. It is not the way of wisdom to attach central importance to beliefs which can never be tested in our experience. A natural theology which builds on experience rather than supernatural revelation must be content to make the most of this life and leave the afterlife in the hands of God.

Other Elements in Chapters 2–4

Before we leave Prov 2 – 4, two passages require a brief comment. First, Prov 3:19 – 20 makes a brief reference to the role of wisdom in creation. Since this theme is developed at length in Prov 8 we may defer the discussion to that chapter. Second, Prov 3:27 – 33 is a brief collection of admonitions which bear on relations with one's neighbor. Such concrete advice is rare in Prov 1 – 9, although it is typical of the rest of

the book. (Prov 6:1 – 19 also deals with specific moral issues.)
The motivation supplied here is religious ("A perverse man is
an abomination to the Lord") but the advice arises naturally
from consideration of what is in a person's best interest. Prov
3:30 is typical: do not quarrel with a man who has done you
no harm. The key to good social relations is reciprocity, or, as
another wisdom teacher said, "as you would that men should
do to you, do you also to them."

The Strange Woman (5– 7)

Chapters 5– 7 consist of a series of admonitions to avoid
"the strange woman." This theme has already come up in
2:16– 19 and will appear again in chapter 9. The sustained
treatment of the theme in Prov 5– 7 is interrupted only by a
brief collection of maxims in 6:1– 19. Since these maxims are
typical of the proverbs in chapters 10– 31 we may comment
on them briefly here before proceeding to the theme of the
strange woman.

Prov 6:1–5: Against Going Surety

The first five verses of chap. 6 stand in some tension with
the usual advice to help your neighbor so that he will help
you. Not only do they advise against standing as guarantor for
someone else's debt, but they are rather frantic about the need
to extricate oneself from such an arrangement. The warning
against going surety recurs frequently– 11:15; 17:18; 20:16;
22:26– 27; 27:13. The underlying thought is most clearly stated in 22:27: "why should your bed be taken from under you?"
For the sages, there are exceptions to every rule, even that one
should help one's neighbor. There is a difference between
charity and stupidity, however well-intentioned the latter
may be. The weight of this advice would obviously vary according to the particular circumstances involved. If the debt
in question were a small one, the anxiety of Prov 6: 1 – 5 would
seem pointless. On the other hand, if the debt were such that
the guarantor could not pay it (as is supposed by 22:26– 27)
then he would be a fool to go surety. Perhaps the main point of
theological interest here is the realism of the advice. Good intentions are not in themselves a virtue. The wise person must
be able to assess a situation realistically and realize what he
or she can effectively accomplish.

Prov 6:6–11: The Ant and the Sluggard

Again, these verses are ruthlessly practical. The sluggard is not credited with detachment from material goods or with trust in divine providence. We might contrast this advice with Jesus' saying about the lilies of the field. No doubt, each point of view is valid in its proper time. There is a limit to what we can achieve by work, but there is no virtue in neglecting to provide for our sustenance.

Prov 6:12–19: Examples of Wickedness

The brief sketch of the man with crooked speech (vss 12 – 15) is undoubtedly a caricature, but a vivid one (he winks with his eye, scrapes with his feet, points with his finger). Such people are not destroyed as suddenly as the sage would have us believe. We must be skeptical of the common assumption in the wisdom literature that nature enforces a moral law. The sage is on surer ground in vss 16 – 19 when he lists seven things which are "an abomination to the Lord." Although they are condemned because "the Lord hates them" they are all eminently human offences which disrupt society. Such conduct is in nobody's best interest, even if its perpetrators are not suddenly destroyed. (The form of these verses—six things the Lord hates, seven are an abomination to him—is especially characteristic of chap. 30 and we will comment on it in that context.)

Chapter 5: Against Adultery

The remainder of chaps. 5 – 7 deals with the "strange woman." (The Hebrew adjective, *zarah*, could be translated "foreign" but the sense here is clear enough. She is an adulteress, another man's wife. The RSV translates "loose woman.") The discussion of this figure in Proverbs vacillates between extremely practical advice on the dangers of adultery and a more symbolic treatment which sees the adulteress as the representative of Folly in all its forms, and so as an anti-Wisdom. The contrast between Lady Wisdom and Dame Folly is fully explicit in chap. 9.

Prov 5:1–6: Adultery as Death

The opening verses of chap.5 are concerned with more than actual adultery. The warning that "the feet of the adulteress go down to death" may seem to be overstated—people guilty of adultery do not necessarily die sooner than anyone else. The sages, however, are not concerned here with physical death. We have seen earlier that "life" in Proverbs is the fullness of life, the intensity of the quality of life. "Death" is the opposite of this. The themes of "life" and "death" in Proverbs refer to the human quest for satisfaction, fulfillment, or, to use the theological term, salvation. From time immemorial people have tried to find this fulfillment in the excitement of sex. (Many examples can be found in ancient mythology.) This theme is clearly present in the Adam and Eve story in Genesis. The serpent in Gen 3 tempts Adam and Eve to eat the forbidden fruit by telling them that they will not die but will become like God knowing good and evil. They do not, however, become like God. When their eyes are opened all they see is that they are naked and they become ashamed. The sexual overtones of the story are obvious but its implications extend beyond the subject of sex. Any human aspiration to become like God is doomed to frustration, no matter how attractive it may initially appear. Prov 5:1 – 6 also plays on the deceptive lure of forbidden sex. The lips of the adulteress drip honey and her palate is smoother than oil. In short, she promises the fulness of life. But in the end she is as bitter as wormwood and what she provides is death.

5:7 – 23   We should not conclude from this that the sages had a negative attitude to sex. They see all the difference in the world between sex in the context of marriage, which takes place within clearly defined social boundaries, and illicit sex, which offers the lure of transcending the restrictions of society in an ecstatic experience. The arguments against illicit sex are varied, but we may note at the outset two basic considerations. In typical wisdom fashion, adultery is not simply condemned by divine prohibition, an imperial edict to be accepted without reason. Rather it is criticized because it is not in our best interest. Second, there is no trace of any asceticism or squeamishness about sex. (Notice the length at which Proverbs dwells on the subject!) There is no talk of defilement or impurity, and no aversion to physical pleasure. The reasoning of Proverbs is not metaphysical. It is simply a reflection on what is good for individuals and society.

An initial consideration, in 5:7 – 14, is the *wastefulness* of adultery. It is possible that the sage is thinking here of the penalty to be paid if one is caught — one might be ruined in the midst of the entire congregation (5:14). There is a deeper consideration, however: "should your streams be scattered abroad, streams of water in the streets?" (5:16). On the one hand, children were considered an unlimited blessing in the ancient world. Adulterous sex was wasteful since it did not contribute to the growth of one's own family. This consideration would, of course, lose some of its force nowadays when zero population growth is seen as a desirable goal! But there is another factor which has lost none of its relevance. Promiscuous sex does not build enduring relationships. A beloved wife is there when you need her, at all times (5:19). We will see in the concluding chapter of Proverbs that the ideal wife provides much more than sexual excitement. There are also the more lasting values of support and companionship. Prov 5:18 – 19 shows that the sages also appreciated the sexual aspects of marriage, but within the context of a faithful relationship. The excitement of adultery is wasted since it does not build the reliable fidelity which ultimately yields the greater enjoyment in life.

Two brief comments may be added before we leave chapter 5. First, in vv. 20 – 22 the threat of divine punishment is introduced as a deterrent for the adulterer. We should not think of this as a divine or extraordinary intervention. The God of Proverbs is not a miracle worker who dramatically interrupts the laws of nature. Rather he is the God who makes the laws of nature work. The Divine punishment of the adulterer need not be distinguishable from the "natural" consequences of the act. If adultery leads to bad results, that in itself is divine punishment.

Second, we might note the metaphorical character of much of the chapter (e.g. "drink water from your own cistern"—5:15). The sages are not merely using euphemisms for sexual subjects—such figurative speech is used throughout the book. Like any good preacher, they know that even such a fascinating subject as adultery can become boring, and so they constantly search for new ways of putting things. In order to get one's point across on a familiar subject it is often necessary to "de-familiarize" it, to put it in a novel way which catches the attention and shows some new aspect of it. We

will see much more of the use of metaphors and analogies as
we go through Proverbs.

6:20–35   In chap. 6 we find another consideration on the
folly of adultery. The adulterer risks blows and dishonor, for
jealousy kindles the wrath of a man (6:33). The sages do not
moralize as to whether jealousy in such circumstances is a virtue or a vice. It is sufficient that it is a fact. The relaxed sexual
ethics of the 1960's and '70's often show a sadly naive view of
human nature in this respect. The jealousy of the deceived
husband (or wife) is not the only factor, of course. While "a
harlot may be hired for a loaf of bread" the consequences of
the act may be far more complicated. Sexual encounters can
arouse the deepest human emotions which cannot be casually
set aside. A philosophy of casual sex fails to reckon with the
depth of these emotions or with the damage that can be in-
flicted when one party is serious and the other is not. The proverbial metaphors of carrying fire in one's bosom or walking
on hot coals (6:27– 28) are apt.

Chapter 7: The Seductress

Chapter 7 provides an extended example of a gullible
youth seduced by an adulteress. The conclusion that her house
is the way to Sheol (7:27) suggests that here again adultery is
being used as a paradigm of all the false human aspirations to
fulness of life. This is not to say that it is a mere allegory. Adultery is a concrete example of the "way of death" just as a faithful married relationship is a concrete example of the kind of
fulness of life that humans can hope to enjoy.

Prov 7 does not add anything to the critique of adultery in
chapters 5 and 6. The more vivid story, however, draws our attention to a motif less obvious in the other chapters: the woman is portrayed as the active seductress while the man is the
gullible victim. This casting of roles is typical of ancient literature—Adam and Eve provide the classic example. Yet there
is no good reason why the roles should not be reversed, and
there is no theological justification for any inference that
women are more responsible for sexual sins than men (see Hos
4:13– 14). The repeated casting of woman as seductress may
to a certain extent reflect the practice of prostitutes, ancient
and modern. More fundamentally, however, it reflects the
male viewpoint which is instinctively assumed in ancient

literature, biblical and other. (The story might be told differently if it were addressed to "my daughter" rather than to
"my son"!) A modern application of Prov 7 would need to re-
cast the story in the light of contemporary customs and mores
and be more sensitive to the respective roles of male and
female.

The discussion of adultery in chaps. 5 – 7 offers rich material for the modern preacher. Adultery, like the poor, we have
always with us. There is no problem of relevance here. However, the simple commandment "Thou shalt not commit adultery" no longer carries much weight, even within Christian
circles, in these days of situation ethics. The reasoning of Prov
5 – 7 does not depend on divine commandment, but shows
how the subject can be approached in very practical terms.
The metaphorical use of adultery in these chapters is also instructive. It can be used to suggest how the prevailing attitudes to sex, which are always a subject of lively interest, can
be used to illustrate and explore broader theological questions of the nature of fidelity, salvation and fulfilment in life.

Wisdom, God and the World (8)

Chap. 8 provides an extensive presentation of personified
wisdom. As in chap. 1, she is said to cry out in public places.
Wisdom is an invitation offered to humanity in all areas of
life. It is not confined to cult or church or to any particular
creed. It is primarily a matter of knowledge and understanding (vv. 9, 12, 14) but it is not coldly rationalistic. We are told
that wisdom *loves* those who *love* her. The emotional depth of
the expression should not be missed, since it goes hand in
hand with the personification of wisdom as a woman and the
contrast between Lady Wisdom and the adulterous woman in
chap. 9. The sages of Israel make no separation between the
emotional involvement of love and rational understanding.
Love, or faith, which is void of understanding is mere folly.
True understanding of what is good finds its natural fulfilment in the commitment of love.

People may be said to love wisdom in so far as they fully
commit themselves to understanding the world they live in, in
all its dimensions. Wisdom may be said to love people in the
sense that it provides the fulfilment they seek. Prov 8 expresses the response of wisdom as the gift of wealth and full

treasuries (8:21) but the wealth could presumably take the form of intellectual and emotional fulfilment as well as prosperity. In any case, the gift of wisdom is more than wealth— "my fruit is better than gold, even fine gold, and my yield than choice silver" (8:19) and instruction should even be taken instead of silver (8:10). Wealth and prosperity illustrate the fulfilment that wisdom brings, but that fulfilment does not depend on them. Wisdom is still the fear of the Lord, which rejects pride and arrogance (8:13). Whatever it may offer, it does not permit anyone to boast.

Prov 8:22–31 provides a quasi-biographical account of the origin of wisdom. We need not concern ourselves here with the mythological roots of this passage. It is quite obvious that we are dealing with a personification. Wisdom is not a separate distinct being. It is rather a quality or an attribute which requires a subject. In view of wisdom's role in creation we should most naturally think that it is an attribute of God. (Compare 3:19: the Lord by wisdom founded the earth.) On the other hand, from the human point of view, wisdom is encountered in the world. It cries out on the heights and city gates (8:1–2) and its association with the different areas of creation in vv. 22–31 suggests that it can be found in those places. So, in so far as wisdom is found in the works of creation, it can be said to be an attribute of the world. Wisdom is not identified with either God or the world. (It was established before the world [8:22–23] and so has a higher status.) It does, however, form a bridge between the creator and creation. It is something which in some way they share and have in common, and which humans, who are constantly urged in Proverbs to "acquire wisdom," can share too.

This discussion of personified wisdom is surely the closest approach to metaphysics in the book of Proverbs, and probably in the Hebrew Bible. What significance does it have for the modern preacher? It bears directly on the way we speak of God. Much of the OT, and of Protestant (more than Catholic) theology, has been marked by a rugged insistence on the transcendence and otherness of God. At the same time, it habitually speaks of God in personal (and specifically masculine) terms, and envisages very direct communication between God and humanity, on the model of human speech. (See our comments above on Prov 1.) The figure of Wisdom in Prov 8 suggests a different approach. In one sense, indeed, the figure of Wisdom seems to come between humanity and God. Our contact with God is indirect, mediated through the created world. Our experience is experience of the world around us. In that world we can find wisdom—the order that satisfies our desire to know and understand. In that wisdom we recognize the wisdom of God, but that wisdom, or the wise order of the universe, cannot be taken as simply identical with God.

Also, while we can speak of wisdom in personal terms, the personification is obviously a figure of speech. In this respect, then, the concept of personified wisdom can serve to remind us of the limitation of the traditional anthropomorphic view of God. The indirect character of our knowledge of God should make us more hesitant to speak in God's name or to claim divine authority for our views. The limited ideas we have about God are inferred from our experiences of the world. We might be well advised to follow the example of the sages by discussing our experience of the world in secular terms and not jumping too hastily to speaking of the divine.

We should not think, however, that wisdom creates any barrier between God and humanity. On the contrary, wisdom affirms that there is indeed continuity between the world we experience and God. Human wisdom is in some measure a participation in divine wisdom. The implications of this idea are considerable. Humanity does not have blindly to obey God or believe mysterious doctrines. Right conduct and truth are based on a rational order which is accessible to us, even if only in a limited way. So we can hope to understand the world around us, and in doing so, to understand God's creation. Human reason is fallible, to be sure, but it is still the most reliable guide we have to ethics and doctrine. The implications for the preacher are clear. It is not enough to proclaim the will of God or revealed doctrine with prophetic fervor. We must also explain and give reasons. To do that, of course, it is not enough to have faith: it is also necessary that we ourselves *understand*.

A further point is related to this. Prov 8 affirms without qualification that the created order is good. If we at all find wisdom, we must find it in and through the created order. The place of wisdom is in the inhabited world and with the children of men (8:31). It is true that a book like Proverbs has little

to say about the problem of evil. Other parts of the Bible speak
far more directly to that issue. The attitude of Proverbs is that
the world is good, if we properly understand it. Evil is not inherent in the order of creation, but results from human ignorance and the lack of wisdom.

Prov 8 concludes with an affirmation that it is indeed possible to find "life" in this world, but it also warns that such
"life" is not automatic. It is found by those who find wisdom,
who walk in the way of wisdom and the fear of the Lord, as
this is described throughout the book. Those who miss wisdom find "death" and injure themselves. So, despite the thorough goodness of the created order, it is possible to miss one's
goal. The theme of the two ways persists. These contrasting
ways are again outlined in chap. 9.

Lady Wisdom and the Foolish Woman (9)

Chapter 9 falls naturally into three sections. Verses 1 – 6
present a new formulation of the call of wisdom. Verses 7 – 12
consist of commonplace maxims, chiefly in criticism of "scoff-
ers," with a reminder that the beginning of wisdom is the fear
of the Lord. Verses 13 – 18 describe the foolish woman. The
main interest of the chapter is evidently focused on the contrast between the two female figures.

The contrast in chap. 9 shows clearly that there is more at
issue in the passages that speak of the strange or foolish woman than the specific sin of adultery. This woman represents a
whole attitude to life, just as Lady Wisdom does. This is not to
say that the adulteress is an allegorical figure or that adultery
is not condemned on the literal level. Rather the adulteress is
a significant example and provides a concrete instance of the
way of Folly. This way, which is also the way of death, is modelled by the adulteress, just as the way of wisdom is modelled
by the faithful wife in chap. 5 and again in chap. 31. The
choice of female figures is significant too. From the uncriti-
cally male viewpoint of Proverbs, the female figures are objects of desire. The chapter holds out two ways of life which
can engage people with the full emotional and existential
depth of sexual attraction. Proverbs does not deal with mental
theories, but with human experience in all its fulness.

The two figures in chap. 9 are deceptively alike. As the
Greek philosopher Socrates knew, humanity always seeks *the*

good. Even the most perverse objectives are seen as good in some respect by those who pursue them. The foolish woman seems to offer "life" in its fulness, just as Lady Wisdom does. The same point is made in the Adam and Eve story in Genesis—they eat the forbidden fruit in the hope that they will be like God and live forever, but in fact it is the fruit of death. In Prov 9, both figures offer bread and drink, the staples of life. (The wine of wisdom suggests a higher quality than the water of Folly, but water too is a common symbol of vitality in the Bible.) There are however two differences. First, wisdom is said to have built a house (9:1). The house is an image of security and shelter, which are values that are always associated with wisdom. Second, the foolish woman offers an additional enticement: stolen water is sweet and secret bread is pleasant. In contrast to the security and contentment offered by wisdom, we sense here danger and excitement, of the particular type that can only be found by transgressing stable relationships. Wisdom places no value on danger (at least, no positive value). It is not opposed to excitement (see 5:18–19) within stable relationships. But for wisdom the highest value, "life," is not a matter of excitement or of transcending the human condition. It is rather a matter of finding contentment within the limitations of the human condition, especially by *fidelity* in established relationships and the trust and mutual support that is so fostered. The excitement of the adulteress does not build a house. It only scatters one's resources and is ultimately not "life" but "death."

We should not conclude from this that the "house" of wisdom offers easy comfort or enjoyment. No house is built without laborious work. Fidelity and trust must be carefully nurtured over many years. Stolen water and secret bread may often come far more easily. Wisdom takes the longer view, which often requires patience and sacrifice in the present. The ability to take such a longer view of what ultimately has the better results is a far better test of the worth of a preacher (or anyone else) than the ability to excite with the prospect of short-term advantage.

Chap. 9, like chaps. 5–7, offers ready material for the modern preacher, though it is not without its pitfalls. No subject has been more abused by Christian preachers than sex. Prov 9 should not be used as an occasion for an old fashioned tirade against "sins of the flesh" or "loose women." The message of the chapter is essentially positive—the value of fidelity. Fidelity is not only a value in sexual relationships, but is the cement of society in all its aspects. The imaginative preacher must seek out a variety of issues where fidelity is at stake, and keep the issue of sex in its proper perspective.

Advice for All Seasons
(Proverbs 10:1–22:16)

This long collection of sayings is introduced simply as "the proverbs of Solomon." The material in these chapters is not organized in any clearly thematic way, although we do occasionally find clusters of proverbs which deal with related subjects. Our procedure will be to pull out those concerns which are most prominent in the different chapters. In doing so we will simply pass over some of the more isolated sayings and not repeat our comments every time a theme recurs in subsequent chapters.

Can the Righteous Go Hungry? (10–12)

The greater number of the sayings in chaps. 10–12 may be grouped together under the rubric "guidelines for a successful life." Some of the maxims are of an obvious practical kind, verging, we might say, on the banal: "A slack hand causes poverty, but the hand of the diligent makes rich" (10:4, cf. 10:5). "Better a man of humble standing who works for himself than one who plays the great man but lacks bread" (12:9, cf. 12:11). The only comment we need make here is on the significance of including such material in a book of biblical wisdom. The goal of wisdom is fulfilment in life, and that definitely includes "bread!" Piety, or even righteousness, is only considered to be a goal in so far as it contributes to the total well-being of the person or community. That well-being is also served by the practical skills involved in making a living and they are just as important for wisdom as the more idealistic aspects of religion.

A conspicuously large number of the sayings in chaps. 10–12, however, take on a rather doctrinaire tone. As typical examples we may take Prov 10:3: "Yahweh does not let the righteous go hungry, but he thwarts the craving of the wicked" or Prov 10:22: "The blessing of Yahweh makes rich and he adds no sorrow to it." (The Anchor Bible takes the second part of 10:22 differently: "and painful toil can add no more.") Similar sentiments are found in 10:27– 30; 11:3– 8,21; 12:3, 7, 12, 21. Classic expressions of this mentality are found in Ps 37:25 ("I have been young, and now am old; yet I have not seen the righteous forsaken or his children begging bread") and on the lips of the friends of Job (e.g. Job 4:7– 8; 8:8– 22). We may detect in these sentiments the rather offensive complacency of the well-to-do. More fundamentally, the sayings ring hollow. The psalmist may have never seen a righteous man go hungry, but if so he cannot have looked very far. The sayings of the sages must always be measured against the evidence of experience, and these particular sentiments have been found wanting ever since the book of Job.

Why then do these doctrinaire pronouncements enjoy such prominence in the book of Proverbs? Some scholars would argue that they represent a secondary layer in the book, which was added to the practical, experiential proverbs, to make them more "religious." This may well be true, but it does not make them any less problematic. In fact it is easy enough to see how these sentiments could arise in the wisdom tradition. Since the sages were convinced that righteousness was indeed in the best interest of humanity, and since human benefit is very commonly measured in terms of material prosperity, it was easy to assume that righteousness *must* lead to riches. However, if there is one lesson above all others that we should learn from the wisdom tradition, it is that nothing *must* conform to our expectations. If we base our theology on experience rather than on dogma, we must take reality as we find it, even if we find that the righteous do go hungry on occasion. Job reproached his friends for "speaking falsely for God" (Job 13:7) when they tried to insist that suffering *must* be a punishment for sin. They were trying to impose a dogma, even when it did not square with experience, and so in effect were being less than truthful about the world as they found it. The same reproach can apply to the moralizing sayings of Proverbs.

What is the modern preacher to do with all this? First, if a preacher is truly informed by biblical wisdom, it is more important to follow the principles of wisdom's appeal to experience than simply to repeat the proverbial sayings in dogmatic fashion. Second, in dealing with any book of the Bible we must be prepared to read and preach *critically*. Biblical books will not always edify us or give us examples to imitate. They can also shock us (think, for example, of the sacrifice of Jephtah's daughter in Judg 11:34 – 40!) or stimulate us to question values and ideas which were taken for granted by the biblical authors. So, in the present case, the prominence of a doctrinaire theory of retribution in Prov 10 – 12 might serve to warn us how easily religious people slip into this sort of moralizing and succumb to the temptation to "speak falsely for God." In short, the best lesson a preacher can learn from sayings like Prov 10:4 or 10:22 is to avoid this sort of facile dogma.

Is it possible to salvage any positive wisdom from these sayings? A clue is provided by those passages in Prov 1 – 9 which used material goods as images for the fulfilment offered by inspiration. So, righteousness may not always keep a person from physical hunger, but it provides a contentment that satisfies the hunger for fulfilment. The blessing of the Lord might be said to give a *spiritual* wealth, which cannot be touched by any sorrow because of the depth of joy it involves. Now it is obviously much more difficult to measure spiritual wealth than material riches, and so we cannot easily verify the sages' claim. We may also doubt whether all criminals are as unhappy as the sages would have us believe. But can we at least say that righteousness brings a contentment which is so completely satisfying that we can experience it as wealth, prosperity, "life" and well-being in the fullest degree?

Here we touch on a very important aspect of wisdom. Righteousness is not only conformity to a set of laws or moral guidelines. It is *by definition* that which satisfies the human quest for life. To be sure, righteousness involves right conduct towards others, fear of the Lord, and the way we perform in life. But it also involves the *spirit* in which we perform. Righteous conduct which is performed in a grudging or resentful way is not the righteousness of wisdom. Wisdom requires a glad heart, and therefore demands that we find contentment in what we do. The frequent assertion of Proverbs that "in the path of righteousness is life" (12:28) can only be maintained if we are able to find "life" and fulfilment in the practice of righteousness itself.

The rewards of righteousness, then, can be positively appreciated, at least as metaphors for spiritual and psychological fulfilment. It is somewhat more difficult to find a positive value in the eager anticipation of the destruction of the wicked. The thought that "the wicked will not dwell in the land" (10:30) or that they will perish with the passing storm is open to objection on two counts. First, it is unrealistic and second it is resentful, if not vengeful—it seems to suggest that our happiness is only complete if we can contrast it with the unhappiness of our enemies.

Both of these objections are substantial. The statements of Proverbs are neither simple truths nor moral ideals. However, the proverbs are not without value. First on the question of realism, the proverb that says "when a wicked man dies his hope perishes" (11:7) points to one of the most basic aspects of the common human experience—the inevitability of death. True, death is just as certain for the wise as for the wicked. (Proverbs does not envisage retribution after death.) The knowledge that whatever we acquire will eventually be lost does not in itself show that righteousness is superior, but it does, negatively, remove one of the most persuasive arguments for crime. Crime is not ultimately any more profitable than virtue. The virtuous man does not lose out, and he has no reason to envy the criminal. So, even though the wicked are not always struck down in mid-career, whatever advantage they enjoy is transitory. The choice between virtue and crime does not depend on the profits of each (since all profits are lost at death) but on the inherent satisfaction that they give. We will find a much fuller treatment of this issue in Ecclesiastes.

Second, on the morality of these proverbs, we must note that on the whole, the tone of chaps. 10–12 is not vengeful and shows no fanatical zeal for persecuting the wicked. Instead the sages counsel humility (11:2) accepting correction (12:1,15), patience (12:16), kindness (11:17), and above all restraint in speech (10:14, 19; 11:12–13; 12:23). However clearcut the distinction between the righteous and the wicked may be, the wise man is cautious. It is not his business to judge or condemn individuals. It is enough that he understand. Fools will bring about their own destruction.

Wealth Has Its Uses (13)

Apart from the theme of retribution, which we have examined at some length in chaps. 10–12, the most conspicuous proverbs in chap. 13 deal with wealth and poverty. Sayings on this topic are scattered throughout the book. We will comment on them again in Prov 19. We have already seen that wealth was often regarded as a reward for righteousness and this sentiment is echoed in 13:21 – 22. However, the attitude of Proverbs to wealth and poverty was by no means a simple one. In accordance with human commonsense, wealth is preferable to poverty, other things being equal. The rich man can at least buy himself off (13:8: the second half of this verse, "the poor man does not listen to rebuke," seems to be corrupt. See the note in the Anchor Bible commentary). His wealth is like a strong city (10:15) while the poor have no defense against the hazards of life. A wise man, then, who seeks the full well-being of the human person, will make no apology for preferring wealth to poverty. However, he also realizes that wealth can be deceptive. Wealth that is too easily come by (the Hebrew has "wealth from emptiness," the Greek translation "wealth gained in haste") may just as easily dwindle (13:11). In Prov 11:4 we read that riches are of little value in the "day of wrath"—they do not make anyone immune to the human fate of death, sickness, or the chance misfortunes of life. The sages also reflects on the oddity of human attitudes to wealth—some who have nothing pretend to be rich, others who have plenty pretend to be poor (13:7). Wealth, in short, is often valued more highly by those who lack it than by those who have it and who realize that it is not the cure for all human ills. Finally, despite the tendency to see wealth as a reward for virtue, the sages knew that poverty in itself is no crime, and may not be the fault of the poor. The land of the poor might yield plenty of food, but it is often swept away by injustice (13:23). Proverbial wisdom does not desire poverty, but recognizes it as a fact of the human condition. One should do what one can to avoid it, but it is not the worst of all possible fates and may be preferable on occasion to some forms of prosperity. We will see further reflections on wealth and poverty in the following chapters.

The subject of wealth is often a delicate one for the pastors of comfortable suburban churches. Most Christians prefer to take the promised "hundredfold" (Mark 10:30) now in this time, and take their chances on squeezing through the eye of the needle. Christian witness in the affluent society may

draw more inspiration from the beatitudes and maledictions
of Luke 6 than from the prudent reflections of Proverbs. Yet,
as Qoheleth would say, there is a time for each. The poor are
not always blessed, in any sense of the word, and the promise
of treasure in heaven should not be used to distract us from
the economic realities of the present. The sages' realistic grasp
of the nature of wealth and poverty is an essential prerequisite
for any prophetic pronouncement. Again, wealth is not necessarily corrupt. A rich man like Zacchaeus finds a place of hon-
or even in Luke, the most socially conscious of the gospels
(Luke 19). Nothing is gained by simplistic rhetoric that de-
nounces wealth, any more than by a facile praise of riches.
Money should not be idolized, but neither Christians nor anyone else can accomplish much without it. The sayings of Proverbs can not be used to justify materialism, but they should be
used in conjunction with passages like Luke 6, so that each
can complement the other.

Two famous proverbs in chap. 13 require a brief comment. "Hope deferred makes the heart sick" (13:12). This
proverb does not imply any moral advice. It simply notes a familiar aspect of human frustration and contrasts it with the
joy of a fulfilled desire. We might compare Jesus' parables
about the thrill of discovering a hidden treasure (even on
someone else's land!) or of finding a lost coin or sheep. Disappointment and joy are not easily categorized in moral terms
but they bear very directly on the quality of life and well-
being. They are no less important than morality for the goal of
wisdom, and should be of no less concern to the preacher.

The second famous proverb is in 13:24: "he who spares
the rod hates his son" (22:15; 23:13). We need hardly warn any
modern parent that scripture should not be read as inspired
child psychology. The proverb is only repeating the accepted
cliché of its time. It is typical of all ancient wisdom that learning and education was thought to involve suffering. It is probably true that we learn more from the harder experiences of
life than from the easier. However, discipline is only commended for the results it can achieve; it is not a value in itself.
The severe parent or teacher, or the scolding preacher is not
necessarily the better one. Wisdom requires that we take account of the best methods of training and communication in
our own time and place.

A preacher can best use a proverb such as this as a jumping off point, to discuss the complex problems of contemporary education, rather than accept it as a conclusion in itself.

The Flexibility of Wisdom (14-15)

In chaps. 14 and 15 we find far less doctrinaire moralizing than in 10–12. Themes of righteousness and retribution are present in some of the sayings, but they are put in perspective. Righteousness, after all, is only one aspect of wisdom. These chapters are concerned with the broader issues of wisdom and folly. The tone is not one of moral exhortation but of reflection and understanding.

Nothing is more typical of the wisdom of Proverbs than cautious reflection: "the simpleton believes everything, but the prudent understands where he is going. A wise man is cautious and turns away from evil, while a fool is arrogant and over-confident" (14:15–16). The significance of these sayings can be seen by contrast with other attitudes which are often thought to be religious—blind faith, zeal or passionate commitment. The sages are wary of faith that can too easily slip into credulity, and of zeal and passion which may mask the unreflective haste of the fool. While Proverbs always makes clearcut distinctions between wise and foolish, righteous and wicked, the distinctions are made in rather general terms. Wisdom cannot be easily equated with a list of beliefs or specific actions. Rather, the wise person is characterized by flexibility. He or she is not committed to an ideal which must be rigidly imposed in all circumstances. Rather, the goal is pragmatic: to achieve the best possible results in the varying situations of life.

Consequently, the tone of the sages is very far from the thundering denunciations of the prophets. They know that "a soft answer turns away wrath but a harsh word stirs up anger" (15:1). It is more important to defuse an angry situation than to insist on the rightness of one's point of view. A hot-tempered person only stirs up strife (15:18), no matter how righteous the anger. Further "a tranquil heart gives life to the flesh but passion is a rot in the bones" (14:30). From the viewpoint of modern medicine we should rather say that passionate anger is bad for the heart, but in any case the sages clearly felt that a calm temperament was better both for the individual and for society. Conversely, when a rebuke or admonition is given, the wise person does not resent it but tries to learn from it (15:5, 31 – 32, compare 13:1; 15:12).

We should not conclude from this that there is no place in wisdom for passionate outrage. Passion clearly is not a value in itself, but it may be justified in particular circumstances. The famous passage in Eccl 3 which says that everything has its proper time, is only articulating a fundamental principle of all wisdom. Consequently it is very difficult to say that anything is absolutely good or bad, since its merit will vary from one situation to another. The same sacrifice may be good or bad, depending on the disposition of whoever offers it (15:8). While wealth is normally better than poverty, "a little, with the fear of the Lord, is better than a great treasure with trouble" and "a dinner of herbs, where there is love, is better than a fatted ox where there is hatred" (15:16 – 17). Because of the diversity of circumstances, the sages prefer to avoid absolutes.

In fact, proverbs do not lend themselves easily to absolute assertions. Consider a simple proverb like 14:4: "where there are no oxen there is no grain." There is some general truth in this statement, but it is not an absolute law. Everyone knows that a man with no oxen (or the equivalent modern machinery) could still buy grain. Also, the proverb can be applied to several situations which have nothing to do with oxen or grain, but where certain resources are required if a goal is to be achieved. By taking the particular case of oxen rather than stating a general law, the proverb makes its point more vivid, but also leaves the listener to decide where it should be applied. Proverbs do not attempt to reduce reality to a fixed number of general laws. Rather they attempt to provide particular examples and suggestions which help us to organize our experience in a flexible way. In this respect proverbs resemble the parables of Jesus. Parables are not systematic. They do not claim to fit every situation in life and the hearer is responsible for deciding when they are appropriate and when they are not. The modern preacher can evidently learn from this method of proverbs and parables. It is not our business to lay down general rules for all occasions, but to provide insights which illuminate some situations but do not claim to be absolute or without exception.

In the light of all this it should be evident that wisdom is not so much a matter factual knowledge or doctrinal learning. It is rather the wit which knows when its knowledge is applicable and relevant. The joy of the sage is to make an apt answer and hit on a word at the proper time (15:23). The same goal is appropriate for the preacher. No amount of pedantic learning (nor, we might add, of unlearned piety) can guarantee that skill. It requires the patience to listen, and a ready wit.

Reflections on Poverty

Chap. 14 also contains some reflections on poverty. In accordance with the practical wisdom of these chapters it does not raise the question of retribution. The observation in 14:20 is purely factual: the rich have many friends, the poor have few. In 14:21 and 14:31 we find a new consideration. One who despises his neighbor is a sinner and one who oppresses the poor insults his Maker, but one who is kind to the poor is blessed. Is this simply an appeal to divine law? Not necessarily. The reference to the creator in 14:31 throws some light on the logic of these proverbs. Rich and poor alike are creatures. Both ultimately depend on a power greater than themselves. It is not prudent then to try to exalt oneself over one's fellows. (Compare Jesus' parable of the Unmerciful Servant, who refused to pardon his debtors, even though he was a debtor himself.) The ultimate reason to be kind to the poor is that we share a common humanity and we never know when we ourselves will be in need. The ethic of charity is implied in that same sense of life's uncertainty which impels the wise person to cautious reflection.

How Little We Can Control Our Lives (16)

The sense of human contingency and dependence is the dominant theme of chap. 16. Two of the sayings (16:1, 9, cf. 19:21) are variants on the theme "man proposes but God disposes." 16:1 is especially striking: even the "answer of the tongue," the ability to express ourselves accurately, depends on God. Consequently arrogance and pride are inappropriate for humanity. The proverbs go further: the arrogant are an abomination to the Lord and will be punished (16:5); pride goes before destruction and a haughty spirit before a fall (16:18). As usual in Proverbs, the Lord here is only implement-

ing human nature—the punishment of the arrogant and the
fall of the proud is a result of their excessive self-reliance and
failure to appreciate their limitations. The counsel of the
sages is cautious: "he who guards his way protects his life"
(16:17) and the fear of the Lord avoids evil (16:6).

The most obvious consequence of this attitude is reliance
on the Lord "Commit your work to the Lord and your plans
will be established"(16:3). We should beware however of taking a proverb such as this as a facile solution to the problems
of life. The point at issue in Proverbs is that we cannot always
control our own affairs or guarantee our own success. Success
is a gift from God. But it would be very naive to think that success can be assured by committing our works to the Lord.
Proverbs does not supply such ready-made solutions and no
responsible preacher should do so either. The sages are not
providing a formula for unfailing success but only reminding
us that success is not ultimately in our hands but in God's.
There are no fool-proof formulae which can guarantee our salvation. We may try to be pure but "all the ways of a man are
pure in his own eyes, but the Lord weighs the spirit" (16:2).
We may try to be upright but "There is a way which seems
right to a man, but its end is the way to death" (16:25). Humanity is always vulnerable to its own ignorance. This point
does not only apply to notorious sinners. It is acutely relevant
to all teachers and preachers who undertake to give advice to
others. The greatest folly of all is to be too sure that one
is right. The pulpit does not exempt one from this general
rule.

We can readily appreciate the need for restraint and
humility before God. However, the caution of the sages also
extended to political life. So we find in chap. 16 a series of sayings about the king. Some of these sound very naive to the
post-Watergate generation: "Inspired decisions are on the lips
of a king; his mouth does not sin in judgment" (16:10). "Righteous lips are the delight of a king, and he loves him who
speaks what is right"(16:13). These sayings represent a worthy ideal of kingship, but we should not expect to always find
that ideal realized. Other sayings have a more realistic ring:
"a king's wrath is a messenger of death and a wise man will
appease it" (16:14, cf. 16:15). We may find these proverbs un-
duly submissive, and prefer the bolder, resistant stance of the

prophets. Both attitudes have their time and place. These proverbs seem designed to cope with a situation where the common people have no practical hope of effectively opposing the monarchy. The attitudes bred by such a situation are in no way normative. Proverbs such as 16:13– 14 are not stating what is morally right, but what is practically possible in a particular situation. If a modern preacher undertakes to address the question of attitudes to civil authority, he or she cannot simply take over the attitudes of Proverbs but must ask what is practically the best thing in the new situation.

One other saying in chap. 16 requires comment: "The Lord has made everything for its purpose, even the wicked for an evil day" (16:4). The saying reflects the typical proverbial tendency to accept the world as it is. This attitude has its limitations, since many things in the world need to be changed. However, it also has its wisdom. It resolutely accepts all creation, even the wicked, as the work of God. We may not understand why there should be evil in the world, but in fact it is there, and if we believe in a creator God, then that God is responsible for the presence of evil too. God did not make an ideal world as we might wish it, and there is no point in pretending otherwise. This should not prevent us from trying to change or remove the evil, but it does mean that we should have a certain amount of patience with a world that we ultimately do not fully understand. These sayings may be helpful to the pastor who has to deal with the terminally ill, or other insoluble problems.

The Ambiguity of Human Actions (17– 18)

The ambivalence of human affairs, how the same thing can be sometimes good, sometimes bad, dominates chaps. 17 and 18. The basic idea is evident in 17:1– 2. A "dry morsel"is not normally desirable, but is better than a feast with strife. A slave would not normally take precedence over a son, but it could happen if the slave were diligent and the son dissipated. This principle of the relativity of all things human also underlies the sayings on bribery in 17:8 and 17:23. The first of these has often given scandal: "a bribe is a charming stone in the eyes of him who gives it; wherever he turns he prospers" (cf. 18:16; 21:14). The saying does not actually endorse bribery, but only states the well-known fact that it works. However, it

does not condemn bribery either, and therein lies the scandal
if we expect the scriptures to denounce sin uncompromisingly. We should know by now that Proverbs does not have clearcut catalogues of what is always sinful or always virtuous. The
merit of any action depends on the circumstances in which it
is performed. As 17:23 notes clearly: a wicked person will use
a bribe to pervert justice. But a bribe is not necessarily perverse. In many situations, and indeed whole cultures, a bribe
is no more than the oil which greases the slow moving machinery of business or politics. Its merit will vary with its effect on the human individuals involved. Preachers may find it
easier to have clearcut moral absolutes, but life or morality is
never in fact clearcut. This point is worth bearing in mind
whenever we are drawn to join in the common chorus that de-
nounces the corruption of politics and government.

The ambiguity of life gives rise to another cluster of sayings in these chapters. The person who is hasty in speech is a
fool. "A fool takes no pleasure in understanding, but only in
expressing his opinion" (18:2) and "if one gives an answer
before he hears, it is his folly and shame" (18:13, cf. 17:27).
What is said of the fool in 18:2 is true of all of us to some extent. It is far more gratifying to pronounce definitively even
on questions where we have little expertise than to be silent
and listen to others. The importance of listening is evident in
all areas of life. It is the key to effective communication, and
our unwillingness to listen is the main reason why we commu-
nicate so poorly. These sayings can be applied in many ways.
For the present we may be content with a few points which are
especially relevant to the preacher. It is perhaps a special
temptation for the preacher, teacher or counsellor to feel com-
pelled to give definite answers to every question. In so far as
we are cast in the role of dispensers of knowledge, we feel
obliged to play the role, even if we have no real knowledge to
dispense. It is also a temptation to have a stock of ready made
answers for the various problems people bring to us. Such a
"dispensary theology" is less demanding than the hesitant
process of listening and thinking through each fresh problem,
but it has little value. Better to admit our ignorance from time
to time than to try to reduce all problems to the answers we
have. And if on occasion we must admit our ignorance, Proverbs has a word of consolation: "Even a fool who keeps silent

is considered wise; when he closes his lips he is deemed intelligent" (17:28).

Wealth, Poverty and Human Solidarity (19)

Wealth and poverty again provide the dominant theme of chap. 19. The attitudes expressed are already familiar. Wealth is normally better than poverty (19:4,7) but poverty is better than folly (19:1) or deceit (19:22). Poverty is no crime, but the person who incurs poverty through laziness is a fool (19:15,24). The most interesting aspect of these sayings is the rationale they supply for the evaluation of wealth and poverty. The value of wealth is that it brings new friends (19:4). The problem with poverty is that it drives away one's brothers and friends (19:7). It is possible of course that friends who are attracted by wealth are superficial friends, whose departure is no great loss. The implication of Proverbs, however, is that it is better to have friends of whatever calibre than to be alone. As we will read in Ecclesiastes 4:11, "if two lie together, they are warm, but how can one be warm alone?" Human solidarity is a value in itself, because in John Donne's phrase "no man is an island" and we all need other people at some time. Solidarity is a value even on the superficial level of keeping company. The deeper the solidarity the greater its value. So it is better to be poor than to be a liar who violates the trust of his fellows (19:22: the first half of this verse is disputed but the RSV reading "what is desired in a man is loyalty" fits excellently with our remarks here). It is the same value of human solidarity which underlies 19:17: "He who is kind to the poor lends to the Lord and he will repay him for his deed." The name of the Lord is invoked here to remind us that kindness to the poor is of the essence of religion. The proverb does not specify *how* the Lord will repay, but we should expect from Proverbs that the retribution will come through the natural order of things —e.g., through the inherent satisfaction of human solidarity or through the respect and gratitude earned.

We may note here that the sense of human solidarity is a recurring interest in Proverbs. We are repeatedly told that a foolish son brings grief to his parents (e.g. 19:13; 17:21,25). Again, quarrelling is repeatedly deplored, especially within the family, where it disrupts the closest of human bonds

(19:13,26). In these sayings the sages are not only concerned
with what we usually consider sins against God. The fool who
brings grief to his father may not be even responsible or able
to prevent it. Yet the grief he causes, like the disruptive quar-
rels, is a human evil. It detracts from the quality of life. The
wise man is concerned with such matters, whether they can
be classified as sins or not. The wise preacher should address
such questions too.

What It Means to Acknowledge God (20:1 – 22:16)

A number of allusions to "the Lord" (Yahweh) occur in
chaps. 20 – 21 and these provide an opportunity for reflecting
on the role of God in the proverbs. It should be clear by now
that we cannot expect to find miracles or dramatic "acts of
God" in this literature. Yet the role of God in human affairs is
not diminished. Quite the contrary. The sages see the presence
of God wherever human beings come up against their own
limitations, and that is frequent indeed. Prov 20:24 is typical:
"A man's steps are ordered by the Lord; how then can a man
understand his way?" (compare also 21:30 – 31).

The first step towards religious understanding in Proverbs is to realize how little we know and control. Appearances
are deceptive, and we cannot take what people say at face
value. In part, this is due to deliberate deception, which may
be reprehensible (see 20:23; 21:6,28) or merely amusing
(20:14; "It is bad, it is bad, says the buyer; but when he goes
away, then he boasts). But more fundamentally we all have a
penchant for self-deception; "Every way of a man is right in
his own eyes, but the Lord weighs hearts" (21:2). (In a lighter
vein, compare 22:13; "The sluggard says, 'There is a lion
outside! I shall be slain in the streets!' " (See also 26:13.) Often
it is hard to distinguish between deliberate deception and superficial but honest intentions; "many a man proclaims his
own loyalty, but a faithful man who can find?" (20:6). From
this it follows that we should not hastily jump to conclusions.
It is not given to humanity to be certain of the truth in a clearcut way. In fact Proverbs suggests that we acknowledge and
make room for God by first of all admitting our own uncertainty and ignorance. This point is of fundamental importance for the preacher. We too often assume that religion, or
faith, gives us definitive, certain knowledge, and that we hon-

or God by being dogmatic in our beliefs. The sages, however, insist that our ignorance is at least as great in religious as in other matters: "It is a snare for a man to say rashly 'It is holy,' and to reflect only after making his vows" (20:25) and "who can say I have made my heart clean; I am pure from my sin?" (20:9). It is important too to remember that religious actions and professions of faith are just as deceptive and unreliable as any other. The sages, like the prophets, knew that "To do righteousness and justice is more acceptable to the Lord than sacrifice" (21:3, cf. Hosea 6:6). Sacrifice is a religious act, but it does not guarantee the sincerity of the one who performs it. Similarly, the person who dogmatically claims to know the absolute truth is in fact failing to leave room for God, no matter what he says about his piety. As another wisdom teacher put it: "Not everyone who says Lord, Lord, will enter into the kingdom of heaven."

Any preacher who stands at all in the biblical tradition has an obligation to warn the people that dogmatic faith is not a virtue, whatever its denominational accent. It is the natural tendency to claim certainty for ourselves and pretend to offer it to others. Those who challenge the certainty of the believers are easily dismissed as lacking faith, or being "negative." Yet the great voices of the biblical tradition from Amos and Jeremiah to Jesus repeatedly expose the ambiguity of life and the superficiality of beliefs that are "certain." The modern pastor must do likewise, although the task is seldom a gratifying one and offers little sense of accomplishment.

Truth and justice are not immediately obvious to us, but the sages believe that in time they will prevail: "Even a child makes himself known by his acts" (20:11); "A false witness will perish, but the word of a man who listens will endure" (21:28). This faith of the sages is not an easy one. It does not mean that our own opinions will necessarily prove right, but that things will work out for the best. It also means, that since only God knows what is ultimately right, we must have patience: "Do not say, 'I will repay evil,' wait for the Lord and he will help you" (20:22). This maxim falls short of the gospel exhortation to love our enemies, but it is a definite improvement over any zealot impulse to retaliation.

The acknowledgement of God, then, is only the other side of acknowledging our human limitations. It requires no mys-

ticism or special revelation, but only a realistic appraisal of
the human condition. To acknowledge God is to acknowledge
our creaturehood and dependence. The practical consequences of such an acknowledgement are evident again in the
attitude to the poor: "Rich and poor meet together, the Lord is
the maker of them all" (22:2). Since wealth and poverty are
not absolutely subject to human control, there is the sobering
suspicion that "He who closes his ear to the cry of the poor
will himself cry out and not be heard" (21:13) or that "he who
oppresses the poor . . . will come to want" (22:16). In all of
this there is no question of miraculous acts of God, but the acknowledgement of God and of our own creaturehood reminds
us of our dependence also on our fellow creatures, and our
need for human solidarity.

Two other sayings in chap. 21 deserve comment, if only
because they illustrate the colorful character of many proverbs: "It is better to live in a corner of the housetop than in a
house shared with a contentious woman" (21:9; 25:24), and
"It is better to live in a desert land than with a contentious
and fretful woman' (21:19). The nagging wife is a figure of
comedy all the world over. Here the picture is completed by
the harried scribe who would prefer the roof-top or the desert
where he might have peace to concentrate on his scrolls or
meditate on his proverbs. The sayings are comic, if a trifle
chauvinistic, and they should not be forced into moralism.
Yet, like much of our comedy, they spring from painful human
situations, and the humor may lead us too easily to assume
that such situations are the fault of the wife. In fact, the husband huddled on the roof is no less ridiculous than his scolding spouse and sayings like these are not meant to assign
blame but to evoke sympathy for both partners involved in
the trials of a human relationship.

Neighborly Conduct
(Proverbs 22:17–24:22)

This section, which is introduced in 22:20 as "thirty say-ings" stands apart from the preceding and following chapters. It consists predominantly of direct exhortations, in the imper-ative, unlike the simple statements that make up most of the book. It is also well known that this section of Proverbs is heavily influenced by an Egyptian work, the Teaching of Amen-em-opet, which consists of thirty chapters, contains many of the same themes and even has many verbal similari-ties. The fact that the material drawn from the Egyptian source fits in so well with the style and tone of the rest of Prov-erbs shows the international character of biblical wisdom. The insights of Proverbs do not require any special revelation. They are of the same type as the proverbial wisdom of any other people.

The subject matter of this section is primarily concerned with social relations, or how we act towards our neighbor. We may notice two tendencies. First there is concern for the rights of the poor and afflicted (22:22–23; 23:10–11; 24:11–12, 15–16). The rationale given is the fear of the Lord, in the sense that we have seen it in chaps. 21–22. Quite simply, we do not know what may happen to us in the future. Prov 22:23 and 23:11 speak of the Lord pleading the cause of the poor and helpless. The Lord represents that vast area of life which is not under the control of any creature. There is, of course, no guar-antee that everyone who oppresses the poor will be punished, but they deserve to be. If they encounter any misfortune they no longer have any claim on the sympathy of their fellows. Prov 24:11–12 warns against self-delusion when we try to shirk our responsibilities: "If you say 'Behold we did not know this' does not he who weighs hearts perceive it?"

This tendency in the proverbs might suggest a measure of moral idealism, but it is balanced by another strain of hard re-alism: "Make no friendship with a man given to anger . . . lest you learn his ways" (22:24–25). "Be not one of those who give

pledges"(22:26). The concern reflected in these sayings is not
what we think of as charity, but self interest. However, wisdom never sees any tension between charity and self interest.
The sayings which invoke the rights of the poor are informed
by the realization that we may all stand in need at some time
or other. The sages are concerned with practical results, not
moral ideals. No purpose is served by giving a pledge if one is
not able to pay. To have one's bed taken from under one
(22:27) is not a noble sacrifice, but merely a ridiculous failure
to take stock of one's resources.

Even the higher moral tone of a saying like Prov 24:11
("Rescue those who are being taken away to death . . .") does
not lead to an absolute rule. In a later section of Proverbs
(26:17), we read that "He who meddles in a quarrel not his
own is like one who takes a passing dog by the ears." A person
who rescues one who is being taken to death might well be accused of meddling in another's quarrel. Which proverb takes
precedence? The answer depends on the circumstances. Evidently, the sages' idea of charity does not imply indiscrimi-
nate interference. We must at least understand the situation
properly and be in a position to act effectively. Otherwise we
may do more harm than good.

In short, despite the fact that Proverbs delights in short
exhortations, it does not provide hard and fast rules on anything. It offers no short-cut through the process of analyzing
every situation on its merits.

One final point on the view of charity in these chapters:
While the hard-headed approach of the sages is not as inspir-
ing as a more idealistic approach might be, it leads to a patient and understanding attitude and offers a solid basis for
human relations. So Prov 24:17 tells us "do not rejoice when
your enemy falls and let not your heart be glad when he stum-
bles"—a noble sentiment. The motivation is surprising: "lest
the Lord see it and be displeased, and turn away his anger
from him." Closely related advice is found in Prov 25:21–22:
"If your enemy is hungry, give him bread to eat; and if he is
thirsty, give him water to drink; for you will heap coals of fire
on his head and the Lord will reward you."(This saying is used
by Paul in Romans 12:20 and so should not be too lightly dismissed as the imperfect pre-Christian morality of the OT). In
these sayings we are not exhorted to love our enemies. Quite

the reverse. We may hope to incriminate them further, to increase their guilt before God, if we are kind to them. Yet the practical result of such advice is kindness towards the enemy, whatever its motive. (It has been suggested that the live coals of 25:22 are derived from an Egyptian ritual of penance. In that case the point would be that kindness moves the enemy to repent and punishes him in a constructive way.) True, it is a noble thing to love one's enemies, but love involves the emotions and is not always ours to command. The attitude of Proverbs, which readily acknowledges our feelings of hostility and provides an outlet for them, is surely better than a pretense of love when we feel resentment. In any case, the important point is that we should act kindly. It is quite possible that the motivation of Proverbs might have greater practical success in producing kind actions than the nobler command to love one's enemy.

The first instinct of the preacher is to contrast these proverbs with the teaching of the gospel. Yet it would be a worthwhile exercise to examine the parables and sayings of Jesus from this perspective. The conduct which seems to be approved in the parables does not always spring from the highest motive. We may think of the friend at midnight (Luke 11:5– 8) or the enigmatic case of the unjust steward (Luke 16:1– 13). The practical result matters more than the intention (again, compare the parable of the two sons in Matt 21:28– 32). We can get a fresh grasp on many of the more idealistic passages in the prophets and in the gospels by assessing them from the pragmatic perspective of Proverbs.

Two of the most striking passages in this section of Proverbs are concerned with the mundane matters of food and drink. 23:1– 2 is a warning to restrain one's appetite when invited to dinner with a ruler. The logic of the passage and the related one in 23:6– 8 is based on caution. Neither the ruler nor the grudging man (23:6) can be trusted and so one should be careful to maintain one's dignity and be on guard. There is also a suggestion that indulgence in matters of food is a weakness, which lessens one's ability to deal wisely with a situation. (Compare the longer passage on this theme in Sir 31:12-21.)

A similar point is taken up in the colorful account of the drunkard in 23:29-35. The drunkard is not accused of sin against God. His condition speaks for itself. He himself is the main one who suffers from it. However, his conduct is destructive and evidently incompatible with the wisdom which seeks the well-being of the entire personality.

The relevance of all this for the modern preacher should be clear enough. Our concern is not with a supernatural order and a revealed morality, but with the good of the human person, even in the most mundane matters. The practical effectiveness of preaching is far more important than the orthodoxy or piety of the ideas which are used to persuade. It is better to deal realistically with what is psychologically possible than to repeat lofty sentiments about love that have little bearing on our actual conduct.

The Practical Nature of Wisdom
(Proverbs 24:23–34)

The brief collection of "sayings of the wise" which completes chap. 24 is closely related to the themes of the preceding section. The most striking saying in this passage is in vs. 29. "Do not say 'I will do to him as he has done to me; I will pay the man back for what he has done.' " The sentiment "do to others as you would have them do to you" is basic to Proverbs, but the corollary, that we should repay in kind, does not follow. Retaliation only deepens the antagonism, and so is counterproductive. Here again charitable behavior is based neither on idealism nor emotion but on the hard-headed calculation of what is ultimately in our best interest. A similar logic can be seen in 24:23–24. Partiality and unfairness in judging undermines the basis of society and is ultimately not in anyone's best interest.

Two other sayings in this passage concern the need for prudence and industry. First, 24:27 warns us to get everything ready before we build a house. We may compare the gospel parable about building a tower (Luke 14:28–30). Neither the proverb nor the parable is concerned only or primarily with spiritual matters. Wisdom is equally involved in the building of material houses. Second, the passage on the sluggard (24:30–34) makes the familiar point that no one can hope to prosper without effort. As usual the lazy man is given no credit at all for detachment from material goods. This passage is also of interest as one of the very rare occasions where a sage speaks in the first person. The observations are still quite probably traditional, but the use of the first person reminds us that all proverbial wisdom claims to be ultimately based on experience. By implication, the modern preacher too can feel free to draw on experience both to test the wisdom of the ancients and as the ultimate basis for his or her own theology.

Both this section and the preceding one may be useful for preaching on charity and related subjects, insofar as they lend a realistic perspective to a subject which is often treated with naive sentimentality.

The Tentative, Relative Character of Wisdom
(Proverbs 25–29)

Prov 25:1–10: Two New Testament Parallels

The opening 10 verses of this section are remarkable for containing two passages which are closely paralled in the NT. Prov 25:6– 7—"Do not put yourself forward in the king's presence"—gives precisely the same motivation for humility as Luke 14:7– 11, where the occasion is a marriage feast. Neither passage makes humility an ideal in itself. It is simply a practical way to avoid giving offense to others and risking a snub or humiliation for oneself. Prov 25:8– 9 cautions against taking one's neighbor to court too hastily and recommends that the issue be resolved privately if possible. The motive is not entirely clear, but the point seems to be that the neighbor might be willing to settle the dispute amiably and the one who rushed into court unnecessarily would then be put to shame. Very similar advice is found in Matt 18:15: "If your brother sins against you go and tell him his fault, between you and him alone. If he listens to you, you have gained your brother." In both cases it is better to "gain one's brother" or restore a good relation with the neighbor, than to get involved in public litigation, which at best will lead to broken friendship.

Passages like these, which are closely parallel in both testaments offer a special opportunity to the preacher. They show the basic continuity between OT and NT and fill in the background against which many of the gospel sayings must be understood. The preacher can use passages like these to emphasize the continued relevance of the OT for Christian readers and to develop themes from either testament by using the other.

Prov 25:11–26:28: The Use of Analogy

One of the more obvious formal characteristics of Proverbs is a delight in comparisons. The greatest concentration of analogies in the book is found in chapters 25 and 26. We may take these as an occasion to reflect on the uses of analogies and comparisons. The comparisons we find in Proverbs are mostly one-liners. The parables of the NT are essentially extended comparisons ("the kingdom of God is like . . ."). There is no doubt that analogy is one of the basic tools of biblical preaching.

The most obvious advantage of comparisons is that they clarify a point by appealing to the familiar experience of the listener. "He who sings songs to a heavy heart is like one who takes off a garment on a cold day and like vinegar on a wound" (25:20), or "like clouds and wind without rain is a man who boasts of a gift he does not give" (25:14). Many of the biblical analogies are derived from the experience of the ancient Near East and the preacher must use ingenuity to find the apt analogies for a modern environment. Clouds and wind without rain suggest extreme frustration and disappointment for a parched Near Eastern farmer. Californians may still appreciate the analogy, but it is not very apt for the Pacific North West. In any case the technique is clear. Any farmer who has experienced a drought will get a vivid impression of what is being said here about the man who promises a gift. Similarly, we can vividly imagine what it is like to take off a garment on a cold day. (I write this in Chicago, where "cold" is a wind chill of 50° below). So we get a vivid impression of the effect of songs on a heavy heart. Like the parables of the NT, the concrete illustration from familiar experience can bring home a point with a forcefulness which can hardly ever be attained by direct assertions.

Of course the vividness of comparisons has a certain price. Someone may say that singing a song has nothing whatever to do with undressing in the cold, and this is true. Analogies are not facts. They are not simply true or false. They are not arguments and they do not prove anything. They are only more or less useful ways of putting a point across. If they ring true to the hearer's experience, well and good. If not, we have to try again. Consequently, finding an apt comparison is a matter of wit, and it is all too easy to miss the mark. An inappropriate comparison, like a proverb in the mouth of a fool, is as useless as a cripple's legs (26:7) or reacts on its user, like a thorn that pierces the hand (26:9).

In one respect, then, analogies serve to relate the point
that is being made to our familiar experience. However, it is a
time-honored proverb that "familiarity breeds contempt."
Familiarity poses a special problem in Proverbs. The sub-
stance of the proverbs deals with familiar everyday experience, and the form of the proverb lends itself to repetition and
rote memory. No wonder, then, that proverbial wisdom is often dismissed as banal and cliche-ridden commonplaces. Yet
the use of comparisons and analogies can serve as a powerful
means for overcoming the deadening effect of excessive familiarity. While the comparisons always deal with familiar
things, they relate them in ways that are far from obvious. In
Prov 26:11, the "dog that returns to his vomit" is familiar
enough. To say that a fool who repeats his folly is like such a
dog is not an obvious fact. It is a particularly harsh evaluation
of the conduct of one who is, after all, a human being. The
proverb challenges us to think about the fool and see whether
there is in fact a resemblance. If we agree, we come to a new
perception of the fool. Similarly, Prov 25:19 ("Trust in a faithless man in time of trouble is like a bad tooth or a foot that
slips") is a challenge to think about the faithless man and see
whether the analogies hold. If they do, we again come to a new
perception. The things compared may be familiar, but the
force of the comparison depends on its unusual character. If it
is too obvious, it is banal. Now many proverbial comparisons
have been worn thin by traditional usage. (Remember the
critic who found Shakespeare to be full of worn cliches!) Yet,
the purpose of such analogies is to permit a new way of looking at the fool or the faithless man. The task of the preacher is
to find ways to break through the routine and familiarity. To
do this, it is never enough to repeat the biblical sayings. Instead we must try to imitate the method of the sages and find
fresh analogies to make our points in challenging ways.

Contradictory Proverbs

We have seen repeatedly that Proverbs are not designed
as a stock of ready-made answers. This point is forcefully illustrated in Prov 26:4 and 5. Here in adjacent proverbs we
find directly contradictory advice. Verse 4 gives reason why
we should answer a fool, verse 5 gives reason why we should
not. Either maxim may be valid at one time or another, but

the sage is not about to tell us what to do in any specific situation. We cannot escape the responsibility of thinking our problems through for ourselves. The moral for the preacher is two-fold. We should not expect the Bible to make our decisions for us, and we should not undertake to make specific decisions for others.

The Danger of Complacency

The indefinite, relative character of many of these proverbs underlines again that wisdom does not consist in knowing a set of specific answers. Rather wisdom must work itself out in the ongoing situations of life. We can never sit back and consider our wisdom accomplished, while there are further decisions to be made. Further, we can never be absolutely certain of what is right in every situation. Consequently, when a man is wise in his own eyes, there is more hope for the fool than for him (26:12). Throughout the Bible no vice is more frequently castigated than complacency, whether it concerns being wise, being righteous, or being saved. We need only think of the Pharisee and the Publican. It is not the business of the preacher to assure a congregation that it is saved, but to remind it that there is no definite or assured salvation while the tasks of life are unfinished.

Prov 27: Nothing Is Definitely Fixed or Certain

The themes of relativity and the uncertainty of human affairs are continued in Prov 27. Prov 27:1 states succinctly one of the most fundamental principles of proverbial wisdom: "Do not boast about to-morrow, for you do not know what a day may bring forth." Every living thing is subject to temporality—to the process of change. Further, no one is endowed with knowledge of the future. We may make predictions, but we are constantly surprised by the course of events. The changeability of human affairs is one of the favorite themes of the biblical writers in both testaments, and is repeatedly used to show the dependence of the creature on God. It is God who controls the course of events, and so "the best laid schemes of mice and men" are often in vain. Most importantly, the uncertainty of the future undermines whatever security we try to establish for ourselves. (Remember the rich man in Luke 12:16– 20—"Fool, this night your soul is required of you; and the things you have prepared, whose will they be?"). The biblical God appears to glory in disrupting any status quo that is established and in surprising our expectations. The entire tradition of biblical eschatology warns that *an end* hangs over every human situation and that it will come like a thief in the night. In the words of the Magnificat in Luke 1, God puts down the mighty from their thrones and exalts the lowly. In this respect Proverbs is thoroughly in agreement with the biblical tradition, although similar insights can be found in the wisdom of all peoples (Prov 27:1 is closely paralleled in the Egyptian book of Amen-em-opet.)

From this prespective on the human situation there is obviously never any room for complacency. Wealth may disappear if the Stock Market crashes. Virtue can be eroded by a new temptation. On the other hand there is always room for hope. No condition is so desperate that it cannot change for the better. While the threat of change may disturb the prosperous, it is the breath of life for the oppressed. It is no wonder then that theologians in the Third World find support in the Bible for theologies of hope and liberation.

The reminder of temporality and human transience which we find in Prov 27 does not require that anyone, even the prosperous, live in a permanent state of anxiety. On the contrary, nothing is gained by anxiety. So, in an earlier chapter we were advised: "Do not toil to acquire wealth; be wise enough to desist. When your eyes light upon it, it is gone" (23:4– 5). This saying might call to our minds the sayings of Jesus about the lilies of the field and the birds of the air. Proverbs, however, is keenly aware that people are not lilies or birds and cannot be quite so carefree in their reliance on providence. So Prov 27:23– 27 advises us to "give attention to your herds, for riches do not last forever." There is no illusion here about the value of wealth. It is transitory and it is not an end in itself. But it is useful for acquiring clothing and food. Characteristically, wisdom lies between the two extremes of anxiety and carelessness. Nothing is gained by anxiety, but the sluggard who fails to make provision is a fool.

One other consequence of the temporality of human affairs may be noted. Timing is all important. What is good at one time may be bad at another. Prov 27:14 provides a delightful illustration: "He who blesses his neighbor with a loud

voice, rising early in the morning, will be counted as cursing."
Anyone who has been wakened early by the prayer-calls of an
Arab mosque or the bells of a Christian church will appreciate
the sentiment. Even the best and most pious sentiments can
result in mere irritation if they come at the wrong time (e.g.,
towards the end of a long sermon). As we shall see again in Ecclesiastes, everything has its proper time.

The emphasis in this chapter on the transitory character
of all things human is especially important since it runs
counter to the usual assumptions about biblical wisdom.
Much of Proverbs does indeed lend itself to an ethic of submis-
sion to the status quo, but since no one knows what tomorrow
will bring no status quo is guaranteed permanence. The rich
and the powerful will not be such forever. This idea contains
the seeds of a revolutionary attitude, although it is not developed in Proverbs. This is one of the few places where we can
get a foot-hold in the wisdom literature for a theology of hope
or liberation.

Chaps. 28 – 29: Some Characteristics of the Wise

The remaining chapters of this section offer little that has
not been seen already in the book. They are marked by repeated contrasts between the righteous and the wicked, and assertions that they will each receive proper retribution (e.g.
28:10,13; 29:6). We have already commented more than once
on the naiveté of such strong contrasts. (See above on chaps.
2 – 4 and 10 – 12). Experience shows only too clearly that the
evil man is not always ensnared in his transgression (contrary
to 29:6). When the sages pronounce such simple dogmas they
are falling short of their usual fidelity to experience. In these
cases the modern preacher can best learn from Proverbs by re-
alizing the inadequacy of such dogmas, not by imitating
them.

The positive lessons we can derive from these chapters lie
in the ideal of the wise man that is presented. One notable
characteristic is that he "keeps *torah*" or instruction (28:7, cf.
28:4,9; 29:18). The RSV translates "keeps the law" but the Hebrew does not have the definite article. Un oubtedly the wise
man would respect the law, but the sages never equate wisdom with merely keeping laws or rules.

What is involved here is much broader; it is a willingness

to listen to instruction and learn from it. The wise man who is prepared to listen and learn stands in contrast with the fool "who trusts in his own mind" (28:26). We have commented above (in connection with Prov 17 and 18) on the importance of listening and the folly of hasty speech. This lesson may be repeated here: "Do you see a man who is hasty with his words? There is more hope for a fool than for him" (29:20). Wisdom is not a matter of eloquence or charisma (in the popular, non-theological sense of the term) but of patient listening and understanding. This point is worth some reflection by preachers in setting their priorities.

A second characteristic of the wise which has often been noted in the previous chapters is repeated in 29:7: "A righteous man knows the rights of the poor; a wicked man does not understand (such) knowledge" (cf. 28:27). As we have seen before, the rights of the poor derive from the common creaturehood of all humanity—poor man and oppressor depend on Yahweh for the light of their eyes (29:13). Prov 28:3 adds an interesting twist to this theme: "A poor man who oppresses the poor is a beating rain that leaves no food." Those who oppress the poor are not always wealthy themselves. It is often tempting in these days of liberation theology and revolutionary rhetoric to assume with the Marxists that class conflict is at the root of all evil. We all get a certain satisfaction out of blaming the evils of the world on the big oil companies or multi-national corporations. No doubt these entities deserve a fair share of blame, but in the last analysis the evils of the world are rooted in the individual human heart. Man's inhumanity to man cuts across the boundaries of class, race and creed. The proverb suggests that the oppression of the poor by the poor is the most cruel injustice of all. Here at least we might expect solidarity. The poor should at least realize their common interest and have sympathy for their common misfortunes. Such, however, is not always the case. We may recall here Jesus' parable of the unmerciful servant which also deals with the oppression of one dependent person by another. It is always easier for a preacher to denounce the big corporations and super-powers, at least when they are not represented in the congregation. But often there is an even deeper source of evil more close at hand. The preacher has a more immediate responsiblity to address the injustices that are found within every congregation, even within the same classes, than the global issues over which he or she has very little influence.

Flattery

One other theme in these chapters requires a brief comment. Prov 28:23 declares that "He who rebukes a man will afterward find more favor than he who flatters with his tongue" and 29:5 says that "a man who flatters his neighbor spreads a net for his feet" (see also 27:6). The first of these sayings might be questioned—flattery has been known to advance many a career. Yet it does not always work, and it seldom is in the best interest of the one flattered. The second saying suggests that anyone should beware of a flatterer, since he cannot be trusted. The flatterer will score no points with a wise or perceptive person. The Hebrew word for flatter is to "make smooth." Undoubtedly flattery often smooths social relations and makes them more pleasant for the immediate situation. Proverbial wisdom, however, looks as always to the long-term result. The initial unpleasantness of a rebuke may be better in the long run. Needless to say, this point has direct relevance for the preacher. Flattery may be a seductive way to avoid confrontation in a congregation, but usually everyone is better served by a direct and honest approach.

Diverse Brief Collections
(Proverbs 30-31)

The Skeptical Words of Agur

In chapter 30 we enter suddenly on material strikingly different from that of previous chapters. Significantly, Prov 30 and 31 are not labelled "proverbs of Solomon." Chap. 30 is introduced as "the words of Agur." We have no idea who Agur was. The title of the chapter is usually translated to say that he was "son of Jakeh from Massa." Most commentators think that Massa was a place in northern Arabia, but that is not certain. Besides, the word "Massa" may be simply the Hebrew word for oracle and not the name of a place at all. The interesting point in all this is that Agur may not have been an Israelite. His sayings are nonetheless a part of scripture, even if he was a gentile. Wisdom does not presuppose a special revelation to Israel and valid wisdom can be found anywhere.

It is generally agreed that only the first four verses should be taken as the words of Agur. Even these few lines are difficult to interpret. The translation of vs 1 is disputed. The words rendered as names in the RSV ("to Ithiel, to Ithiel and Ucal") are translated by others as "I am weary, O God, I am weary and worn out" (NEB) or even "There is no God! There is no God, and I can (not know anything)" (Anchor Bible). There are problems with each of these and especially with the last one. No theological weight can be placed on this verse. Some would say that v. 4 is supposed to be spoken by God (compare the speech of God in Job 38 – 41). The text however seems to indicate that vv. 2 – 4 are words of Agur.

The sayings of Agur are striking in their bluntness and are more similar to Ecclesiastes than to Proverbs: "I am more brute than man" (so Anchor Bible, cf. NEB. RSV has "I am too stupid to be a man"). "I have not the understanding of a man." There would appear to be a touch of irony in this self abasement. The understanding which Agur lacks is knowledge of God, and what human can claim to have it? The questions in

v. 4 then are taunting, like God's questions to Job from the storm cloud. "Who has ascended to heaven and come down"—obviously no one. Also only God knows about the works of creation listed in the following questions. These questions are taunting for anyone who claims to be wise. If Agur is less than a man, so are we all. But in fact the ignorance of Agur is essential to the human condition, although not everyone will admit it as readily as the son of Jakeh.

Agur's confession of his human limitations seems thoroughly compatible with the wisdom we have seen throughout the book of Proverbs (e.g. chap. 16) even if it comes from a different source. It is only skeptical about things which lie beyond the range of human knowledge, and does not necessarily despair of the normal competence of the intellect. It does, however, clash with any claims of revealed supernatural knowledge. Agur would obviously be skeptical of a prophet who proclaimed absolute truths as the word of the Lord.

Prov 30:5–6 highlights the clash between the skepticism of Agur and the claims of revealed religion. These verses are generally thought to have been inserted by an editor, as a corrective to Agur by insisting that there are revealed words of God which provide definite knowledge. Such an appeal to the "words of God" is quite out of character for Proverbs. It is interesting that v. 6 adds a warning "do not add to his words" which looks like an attempt to close the book of Proverbs and declare it canonical scripture. We will find a similar editorial comment at the end of Ecclesiastes.

What is the modern preacher to make of the conflicting attitudes of Agur and the sage of vv.5– 6? The issue is an important one for the nature of preaching. From the perspective of Agur, no preacher has been to heaven, and so we must all present our views as fallible human opinions. Vv. 5– 6 might suggest that we can preach not our own views but the definitive "words of God." But what are the "words of God" to which v. 5 refers? Presumably the scriptures. Christians have always held that the scriptures may indeed be called the "words of God" but they are also human words. Biblical revelation is mediated through the words and actions of human beings who are conditioned by the particular circumstances of their time. The book of Proverbs is itself an example of the canonical "words of God." We have seen repeatedly how even the most profound insight is constantly shown to be relative and will vary in significance from one situation to another. Even if we are disposed to grant that some prophets and visionaries may have "gone up to heaven and come down" the preacher is left to decide how their words fit any particular situation. There is no justification, then, for preaching as if our message were guaranteed from heaven. No preacher (or expositor) can offer more than fallible human insights or fallible applications of scripture. It is far better to admit this at the outset than to try to play the role of definitive spokesman for God. The wise preacher, like the rest of humanity, would do well to take the skepticism of Agur to heart.

Prayer for Moderation

The editorial defense of the "words of God" is followed by a prayer which is thoroughly in the spirit of the wisdom tradition (30:7–9). Two things are prayed for: "Remove far from me falsehood and lying; give me neither poverty nor riches." The latter part of the prayer is especially interesting. Wealth has its temptations, to be sure, but it is not the root of all evil. Poverty too can be an occasion of sin and implies no virtue in itself.

Numerical Sayings

The most striking characteristic of chap. 30 is the frequency with which proverbs are introduced by a number or numbers. In Prov 30:7,15 and 24 we have a single number ("Two things I ask of thee...") but the more characteristic form is that found in 30:15–16, 18–19, 21–23, 29–31: "Three things are never satisfied, four never say 'Enough' " (30:15). Two points should be noted. First, even though these proverbs always list precisely *four* things, the three... four pattern suggests an indefinite number. In Prov 30:18 it is by no means implied that there are *only* four things that the sage does not understand. The proverb illustrates the limits of his knowledge, but it could also be illustrated in many other ways. Second, the four things listed are in effect being compared. They are said to have something in common. The items in question do not form an obvious class. In fact, the point of the proverbs would seem to be the surprise that the four can be compared at all. A proverb like Prov 30:24–25 could easily be converted into a riddle to tease the wit of the listener—"what do these four things have in common...?" In at least some cases the comparisons throw a new light on the last item in the list. So, the way of a man with a maiden is mysterious as the way of an eagle in the sky, and a maid who succeeds her mistress is like a fool who is filled with food.The force of such a comparison is most clearly evident in Prov 30:29–31; the stately stride of a king can be compared not only to the lion but also to the strutting cock and the he-goat. (The translation of this verse is not certain—see the notes in the Anchor Bible.) Like all analogies and comparisons, these ones are not necessarily compelling. They are suggestions of ways of looking at things, and we may find them more or less helpful.

There is little in these sayings that we would call theological. What use are they for the preacher? Perhaps they may serve to suggest that preaching is not always strictly theological, but, like wisdom, can range widely over human nature and the world. Proverbs like these are musing reflections which try to see the connections and similarities between diverse phenomena, and search for new ways of looking at the familiar things around us. Their goal is not only understanding but also the enjoyment of wit and ingenuity. They do not try to distinguish definitively between right and wrong, but to appreciate a variety of ways of looking at things. From the perspective of proverbial wisdom, such patient understanding is a more worthy goal for the preacher than the ringing pronouncements of right and wrong that are often associated with the pulpit.

The Way of the Adulteress

One isolated saying in chap. 30 deserves comment. In Prov 30:20 we read: "This is the way of an adulteress: she eats, and wipes her mouth, and says 'I have done no wrong!' " The theme of the adulteress has been treated at some length in the opening chapters of Proverbs. Here we only want to reflect on the craft of the saying. The reference to eating is clearly an allegory for sex, but it avoids the possible crudeness of a direct reference. It also suggests that the adulteress treats sex as casually as a daily meal. The picture is far more vivid than could be drawn without the allegory. As in the use of analogies and comparisons, the familiar experience of everyday life (here eating) is used to throw a new and unfamiliar light on the subject in question (adultery). Apt use of allegory and analogy is undoubtedly a gift which is not equally available to every preacher, but it is an invaluable tool if we want to ground our preaching in a solid understanding of everyday life.

Advice for a King (31:1–9)

Prov 31:1–9 is another distinct unit, attributed to one Lemuel, king of Massa of whom nothing else is known. (Some commentators emend the name Lemuel and read "a king acting foolishly.") Massa was *possibly* a tribe in north Arabia, so again these pieces of wisdom may have been gathered from outside the boundaries of Israel.

The advice in these verses is directed to a king. He is warned against excessive indulgence with women and drink, and reminded of his obligations to the poor and needy. Such concern for the needy is a standard theme in wisdom literature and is born of the realization that we all share a common humanity and are vulnerable to the same misfortunes. The most distinctive note in these verses is found in the comments on drink. Strong drink is dangerous for a king "lest he forget what has been decreed." On the other hand, wine is good for those in misery, so that they may forget their poverty and distress. In short, the sage is no prohibitionist. Strong drink has its use. The king is not forbidden to drink by any divine law, but drinks at his own peril because of its effect on his mind. We may hesitate at the recommendation of wine for those in misery. Too often strong drink only adds to the misery of the poor by wasting whatever resources they have and dissipating their energy. Yet, the sages are compassionate here. Drink may not be the best solution for the woes of the poor, but in some cases it may be the best available. Wisdom always requires that we assess what is practically possible. It is not always better to insist on preaching the virtues of industry and hard work (although, as we have often seen, the sages had little patience with the sluggard). There are times when people need not exhortation but sympathy and compassion or even a drink!

31:10–31: The Capable Woman

The book of Proverbs concludes with a long passage that sings the praises of the ideal wife. Most of the references to women in the wisdom literature speak of the snares placed in the paths of men by adulterous and seductive women. It is not unfair to say that these references often now appear as snares in the path of the preacher, confronted with a feminist consciousness that was unknown to the sages. Prov 31 might be taken as an attempt by the sages to redress the balance by giving a positive view of women, but it too has its pitfalls. The "good wife" envisaged by the sages, who looks after the house while her husband takes his seat at the city gate, is not a prototype of the modern liberated woman. A preacher who holds up Prov 31 as an ideal for the women in his congregation can hardly expect to be taken seriously.

How seriously should a passage like this be taken as an ideal? Like all the wisdom of Proverbs, it is not meant as a prescription for all time but as the conclusion from the experience of the sages in ancient Israel. It reflects an ideal which was actually held in one particular culture, not necessarily one that should be held in all cultures. It should be said here that all preachers and theologians who try to derive absolute ideals from the scriptures inevitably realize that some biblical guidelines are dated and no longer applicable. What Christian preacher would now insist on all the purity laws of Leviticus? It is unfortunate that the predominatly male ranks of clergy and theologians have often seemed to treat passages relating to women with a seriousness which is not accorded to all areas of the Bible. In short, Prov 31 can in no sense be taken simply as an ideal for modern women. It must be measured against modern experience to see whether it can still provide any insights that are of value.

However far it may be from a portrait of the "liberated woman," Prov 31 is surely further from the "total woman" of some conservative Christian circles. The emphasis of the chapter is on the *capable* character of the woman. (The NEB translation "capable wife" is more accurate than the RSV "good wife" in v. 10.) She is no mere homebody but an efficient businesswoman. She buys fields and plants vineyards and sees that her merchandise is profitable (vv. 16,18). Far from cultivating a delicate femininity she "girds her loins with strength and makes her arms strong" (v.17). If Prov 31 can be taken to suggest anything about the role of women, it is that they can exercise responsibility quite as widely and efficiently as their male counterparts. The woman portrayed here is active and independent. She is attractive, but she is very far from being merely a sex object or a homebody.

Prov 31 is not simply a job description for the ancient world or the modern. As the closing section of the book it inevitably calls to mind the lengthy discourses on the "strange woman" in the early chapters. We noted above that the "strange woman" was at once a real figure drawn from the experience of the times, and a metaphor for a deceptive and disastrous life-style. The sages warned not only against actual adultery, but against a whole style of life that could be symbolized by adultery. Similarly in Prov 31 the sage is not only portraying the capable woman, but also the way of wisdom, which should be desired and sought like a good wife. The virtues of industry and efficiency are highlighted, but these are not goals in themselves. They are placed at the service of people. Through them she provides for her husband and children. Consequently, her efficiency creates the basis for security and trust (31:11). She is said to have "the teaching of kindness" on her tongue (31:26). The Hebrew phrase here (*torath hesed*) could also be translated "teaching of loyalty." In either case, the point concerns a faithful respect for those around her. This kindness is not confined to the family but extends to the poor (31:20). Her virtues then are in the service of human solidarity, which we have often seen in Proverbs as the converse of the "fear of the Lord."

The contrast with the "strange woman" of the early chapters is, perhaps, most obvious in v. 30: "Charm is deceitful, and beauty is vain, but a woman who fears the Lord is to be praised." The moral, of course, applies to men quite as well as to women. Charm and beauty are not bad in themselves— quite the contrary. Yet they can be deceptive. The pursuit of passing beauty typifies a life oriented to excitement rather than fidelity and stability. Excitement too has its place, but in the way of wisdom it is not the supreme value. It must be subordinated to the contentment born of fidelity which can be defined as the fear of the Lord.

ECCLESIASTES

The book of Ecclesiastes is introduced as "The words of Koheleth, the son of David, king in Jerusalem." The word Koheleth is usually translated "Preacher" but while the contents of the book may be taken as a kind of preaching, the author is not a clergyman or prophet. The precise meaning of the word Koheleth is debated. (Interestingly, it has the form of a feminine participle.) The word is generally thought to mean "one who assembles the congregation." (Ecclesiastes is the Latin equivalent.) At least in the opening verse (which was probably added by an editor) the author is identified as the son of David, Solomon, who would "assemble the congregation" in his role as king. This identification is supported by later statements that he was "king over Israel in Jerusalem" (1:12). The identification with Solomon is, of course, a fiction. The tradition tended to ascribe all wisdom to Solomon (even the so-called "Wisdom of Solomon" which was composed in Alexandria in the time of Christ.) The opening verse only serves to locate the book of Ecclesiastes in the wisdom tradition. This location is correct. Ecclesiastes is often critical and skeptical over against the older wisdom tradition, but we shall see that even its skepticism is founded squarely on the principles of wisdom.

The Power of Negative Thinking (1:2–11)

"Vanity of vanities! all is vanity." This sweeping assessment of the human condition provides the keynote for the message of Ecclesiastes. It is not by any means the sum total of his message. Ecclesiastes is by no means the total pessimist

that his opening sentence might suggest, but the uncompro-
mising insistence that all is vanity is the necessary framework
within which his positive message must be understood.

What does it mean to say that all is vanity? The phrase
"vanity of vanities" has such a time-honored ring to it that
other translations (NEB: "emptiness, emptiness") are weak
by comparison. Unfortunately the familiarity of the phrase
can often cause it to slip past us without making any real impression. The Hebrew words are more accurately rendered as
"vapor of vapors" (so the Anchor Bible). The significant characteristic of vapor is that it disappears, as Shakespeare would
say "into thin air." It is transitory, and so is human life. This
insight is commonplace enough, although it is seldom presented as forcefully as here. In a general way we might compare the famous sayings of the Greek philosopher Heraclitus
that "everything flows, nothing stands still" and that you cannot step in the same stream twice, because it will have
changed already. The theme of the constant flux of all things,
was also fundamental to the biblical tradition. Second Isaiah,
surely one of the most optimistic voices in the OT, reminds us
that "All flesh is grass and all its beauty is like the flower of
the field. The grass withers, the flower fades..." (Isa 40:6–7)
and the entire biblical view of history rests on the insight that
God can bring down the mighty and exalt the lowly with the
passage of time. Awareness of the temporality of human affairs was fundamental to the entire tradition of proverbial
wisdom (see our remarks on Prov 27 above). What Ecclesiastes does here is set forth this common insight with an emphasis and consistency that is without parallel in the biblical
writings.

Certain consequences follow from the transitory nature of
human affairs. First, the question: "what does a man gain by
all the toil at which he toils under the sun?" or more literally,
"what profit has a man?" The word translated "gain" or
"profit" is derived from the Hebrew word for "remainder, ex-
cess." The idea is: what do we have to show at the end of our
labors? The human condition is indeed laborious. Even when
we enjoy our work it is tiring and constrains our freedom. The
common human instinct is to endure the toil of work, not for
its own sake, but for something we will achieve or gain. Ecclesiastes bluntly reminds us that there is no permanent or se-

cure gain. We are reminded again of the rich man in Luke
12:16– 20 who built his barns but never lived to enjoy them.
Any hope of gain or achievement will eventually be disappointed, at latest by death, if not sooner. It is important here
to distinguish between Ecclesiastes' notion of "profit" or
"gain" and his notion of "enjoyment" which we will meet later. Enjoyment is found in the present. It is not necessarily lasting. It cannot be accumulated or deposited in a bank for
future use. It is quite within the possibilities of temporal humanity. Profit, by contrast, is something which is objectifi-
able and can be accumulated and stored. It is something
which satisfies our desire for security and permanence. It is
what Ernst Becker, in his fine study *The Denial of Death* (New
York: The Free Press, 1975) would call an "immortality symbol"—something which seems to be salvaged from the flux of
time and seems to shelter us from the transience of all things.
Ecclesiastes insists that there is no such shelter, that the security and permanence of our profits is an illusion. This does
not mean, however, that there is nothing good in life. There is
still, as we shall see, the possibility of enjoyment.

Further, what is true of gain or profit is also true of
achievement. One of the most common "immortality sym-
bols" is the hope of accomplishing something of lasting value.
While we usually realize that we cannot avoid death, we often
dream of leaving a reputation that will live after us. This desire for fame is inevitably competitive. To have any chance of
being remembered we must stand out from the herd. It is not
enough that what we do is good, it must be better than what
the other fellow does. Ecclesiastes reminds us of the folly of
such hopes: "There is no remembrance of former things, nor
will there be any remembrance of later things yet to happen
among those who come after" (1:11). Even the most famous
names are known only to a small segment of the world's population and few indeed are remembered for more than a few
generations. Further, most human accomplishments only
seem outstanding because of our ignorance of history. "Is
there a thing of which it is said, 'See this is new'? It has been
already, in the ages before us" (1:10). This statement should
perhaps be qualified: the landing of astronauts on the moon
was, to the best of our knowledge, a genuine first. But there
were analogous accomplishments, quite as momentous in

their day (e.g. the discovery of America). The accomplishments of most of us are not in the same category as landing on
the moon, and are far more likely to have been anticipated by
earlier generations. Any biblical scholar who has taken the
trouble to read the literature of the 19th century knows that
many ideas which now appear novel and exciting were already debated a century ago.

It is in this sense that Ecclesiastes tells us that there is
nothing new under the sun. This famous saying should not be
thought to mean that nothing changes—quite the contrary.
What Ecclesiastes rejects is the popular myth of progress.
Each generation likes to think that it has made some decisive
advance over its predecessors. Hence our obsession with keeping and breaking records in sport and our preference for "the
latest" in technology. Now there is no doubt that humanity
has made progress over the centuries in many respects. However, we cannot take the course of human history as an unbro-
ken advance. Elaborate civilizations have crumbled in the
past. No doubt ours will too. More important, there is least evidence of progress in human nature itself. The ambitions and
obsessions which motivate us seem little different from those
known in antiquity. Further, the great advances in human understanding by a Plato or a Shakespeare are not accomplished
once and for all but must be appreciated and understood
anew by every generation. "The eye is not satisfied with see-
ing nor the ear filled with hearing" (1:8). Understanding and
insight cannot be accumulated in libraries and art galleries.
They must be attained by each individual for himself. The
business of civilization is never accomplished but must be
pursued in different forms in every generation.

We have dwelt at some length on the opening section of
Ecclesiastes because it contains some of the basic ideas of the
book. What does it offer to the preacher?

Most obviously, it is likely to offer a problem, in what one
might call pastoral technique. To put it mildly, the tone of the
passage is rather negative. It does not appear to be informed
by any trace of the "positive thinking" which we are often told
is the key to success in business and preaching alike. A modern audience may find such gloomy reflections unattractive, if
not depressing. Would the preacher not be well advised to emphasize the brighter side of life?

Now there is no doubt that positive thinking has its place in preaching. Everyone needs a little encouragement from time to time. Yet it is striking how much of the preaching contained in the Bible is negative in tone. Amos, Jeremiah, Job or John the Baptist could scarcely be described as cheerful, or even optimistic in attitude. We should consider then whether there is not a certain *power of negative thinking* which gives Ecclesiastes its forcefulness. In what does the power of negative thinking lie? First, it is clearly in harmony with the common biblical polemic against idolatry. It undermines the various gods of wealth, power, progress and ego by showing their transitory nature. The critique of human pride and aspirations in both the prophets and Ecclesiastes clarifies the limitations of humanity and the difference between God and man. It reminds us what it is to be creatures, and nourishes the "fear of the Lord."

The negative insistence on the limitations of humanity not only moulds our attitudes towards God but also creates a framework for relations with our fellow human beings. We have noted above that the human desire for achievement and fame is inevitably competitive. The desire to stand out and be remembered is a disruptive force in society which sets human beings against each other. Also the accumulation of "profit" in the form of wealth and power inevitably sets some people above others, and structures society in terms of "more" and "less." The negative critique of an Ecclesiastes reminds us that such distinctions between more and less important people are not essential to humanity. The trappings of power and wealth which distinguish us are ultimately vapor and vanity. At bottom we are all human beings who share a common fate. The bond of human solidarity which unites people in sympathy is a deeper and more important thing than the various rankings by which we are differentiated.

The negative thinking of Ecclesiastes has, then, positive goals. The sense of creaturehood and human solidarity are positive things which can provide the basis for a joyful life. However, it is difficult to speak positively of these values without setting them up as standards, by which we can rate and compare people and assess "profit." Even the best actions can be performed with the self-serving goal of promoting ourselves above others. We are all familiar with the Pharisee who

felt that he was "not like other men" because of his observance of the law (Luke 18). Now the law, as Paul would say, was
holy and just and good, but for the Pharisee in the parable the
works of the law were a means of "profit." This mentality is
what George Bernard Shaw dubbed as "salvationism" (in his
preface to *Androcles and the Lion*). Salvationism is not so
much interested in the value of a particular act in itself as in
its "profit"—ensuring the salvation and exaltation of the one
who does it. The message of Ecclesiastes is that such "salvation" is an illusion, just as Jesus taught that the superiority of
the Pharisee was an illusion too.

In the light of these remarks we may appreciate the power
of Ecclesiastes' negative thinking. It offers no new idols, no
new "salvationism" but rigorously rejects any "profit" we
might claim to find.

The full power of this negative tone should not be lost on
the Christian preacher. Too often Christians dismiss books
like Ecclesiastes as pictures of "man before grace" or "before
the resurrection." Some strands of Protestant theology (for example Karl Barth) have indeed placed great importance on
the abject helplessness of humanity, when left to its own resources. However, the assumption usually is that we as Christians have been rescued from this common human condition.
Ecclesiastes depicts the situation of others, not of us. Now it
should be painfully obvious that such an attitude on the part
of the Christian is perilously close to that of the Pharisee, who
gave thanks that he was not like the rest of men. Christianity
gives us no exemption from the human condition. St. Paul,
who preached the resurrection as fervently as anyone, also
said that those who were baptized into Christ were baptized
into his death (Rom 6). Only those who absorb in some way
the experience of crucifixion and death can hope for resurrection beyond it. Anyone who turns to Christianity as a short-cut
to salvation or to "gain" immortality is suffering an illusion.
In the paradoxical words of Jesus, whoever wants to save his
life must be prepared to lose it. Ecclesiastes might well be
said to depict "crucified" humanity, which has abandoned its
hopes for "profit" and so has lost its life in Jesus' sense. It applies just as fully to the Christian as to anyone else. We will see
that Ecclesiastes also offers a renewed appreciation of life,
which might be described as a kind of "resurrection." The

positive life of Ecclesiastes, however, only becomes possible through the thorough negative rejection of the false hopes of "gain" and achievement.

The Need for Letting Go (1:12 – 2:26)

The remainder of chap. 1 and all of chap. 2 recounts the experiences which led the author to conclude that all is vapor. He presents himself as Solomon, the king of legendary wisdom. So, his reflection is applied to everything associated with the wisdom of Solomon, and becomes in effect a critique of the traditional ideas of wisdom and success. The use of the first person "I" is still significant. The views put forth are the reflections of the sage himself. Ecclesiastes pits his own assessment of experience against the weight of the tradition. He has often been criticized for placing so much weight on his own ideas and refusing to trust the tradition. Yet in this he is faithful to the deepest principles of wisdom. As we saw in the introduction to this volume, wisdom is based on experience, not on revealed dogma. The test of traditional wisdom must always be whether it fits our ongoing experience. An accepted tradition, whatever its origin, tends to harden into dogma. We saw several examples in the book of Proverbs where observations which are true enough in some cases (e.g. that the wicked are punished) were elevated to the status of absolute laws (that they are *always* punished). Such absolute dogmas are very plainly contradicted by experience, and honesty as well as wisdom demands that we recognize the priority of experience over tradition in such cases. This point is made very clearly in the book of Job. When Ecclesiastes insists on testing the dogmas of tradition by his own experience he is not guilty of any lack of faith or trust but simply exercising the responsibility of any honest thinker.

The conclusion reached by the sage is stated at the outset: "it is an unhappy business that God has given to the sons of men to be busy with" (1:13). So, wisdom brings vexation (1:18), pleasure is vapor (2:1), the achievement of surpassing all who had gone before is a striving after wind (2:11). The wise man is forgotten like the fool and one who toils must leave the fruit of his toil to another. Yet in 2:24 – 26 the sage asserts that "there is nothing better for a man than that he should eat and drink and find enjoyment in his toil."

Two problems immediately occur to the interpreter. First, how can Ecclesiastes say that the pursuit of wisdom is mere vanity, without undermining his own position as a sage? Second, how can he say that the pursuit of pleasure is vain, and yet recommend that we eat, drink and find enjoyment? The answer is that neither wisdom nor pleasure are good or bad in themselves. Their value depends on the attitude and motivation with which we approach them. If we pursue wisdom for the sake of becoming famous or of achieving something permanent, then indeed we are chasing after wind. Wisdom has its value; "the wise man has his eyes in his head, but the fool walks in darkness" (2:14). There is an advantage to wisdom in so far as it facilitates the living of life, in so far as we put it to use. But the mere "possession" of wisdom is no "profit" in the end. We still share the same fate as the fool. (The word "fate" here does not imply that all our lives are predetermined, but only that we cannot control what is going to happen to us and that death is inevitable.) A person who labors to excel in wisdom is, in a sense, making an idol of wisdom and perverting it. Such a person endures the labor of study, not for its own sake, but for an end-product which is at best fleeting. Who cares whether Solomon was wiser than everyone else in Jerusalem? If he deprived himself of the enjoyment of life to attain that goal, then he missed out on life, for no good reason. The result of such labors is the frustration which causes one to hate life (2:17). (This verse expresses the outcome of Ecclesiastes' experiments with achievements, not the final message of the book. See further the remarks on chap. 4:1 – 3.) True wisdom, for Ecclesiastes, lies in appreciating the vanity of striving to accomplish. Whoever makes wisdom itself an accomplishment is not wise, but a fool.

The case is similar with pleasure. If pleasure is made an end in itself, so that we work at it and pursue it, then it too is perverted. What Ecclesiastes recommends in 2:24 – 26 is not the pursuit of pleasure but the enjoyment of life as it comes. For that reason he hastens to add that enjoyment is a gift from God (2:24). It is not something we can achieve by working at it. It is like floating. The harder we try the less we succeed. In order to enjoy we must first relax, "let go." We must stop worrying about salvation and "lose our lives" if we are to find them.

The concluding verse of chap. 2 summarizes the thrust of the chapter: "For to the man who pleases him God gives wisdom and knowledge and joy; but to the sinner he gives the work of gathering and heaping, only to give to one who pleases God. This also is vanity and striving after wind." Some commentators have thought that this verse is an editorial addition, affirming that God rewards the just and punishes the wicked. But the verse does not use the words "just" and "wicked." The word for sinner can be taken as "one who misses the mark." Far from affirming a pious dogma the verse shows how Ecclesiastes defines the sinner. Whoever spends his life in "the work of gathering and heaping" misses out on the enjoyment of life, and so "misses the mark," which is what it means to be a sinner. The irony of such a life is that all that is gathered must be left to someone else, and we never know what that person will do. By contrast, the person who can take life as it comes and enjoy it, is the one who pleases God.

The Role of Work

The fruitlessness of toil is a recurring refrain throughout this section. Ecclesiastes is well aware of the necessity of work. So in 2:24 he recommends that we find enjoyment in our work. It is folly, however, to undertake unnecessary labors in the hope of achieving fame or lasting profit. Labor is the human condition. It is the business God has given us to be busy with (1:13), and in some measure it is necessary not only for enjoyment, but for survival. We should not however think that by adding to our labors we can add to our stature in any permanent way. (Compare the saying of Jesus in Matt 6:27.)

The preacher should have no problem in discovering the relevance of these chapters to the so-called "work-ethic" which is often said to be typical both of Protestantism and of American society.

A Time for Everything (3:1–15)

We have already seen on a number of occasions in Proverbs that wisdom is not simply the knowledge of what is right or wrong, but rather lies in the timing, since the same thing may be good or bad on different occasions. This principle is most clearly set out in Eccles 3:1– 8. Here again Ecclesiastes takes a point that is deeply embedded in the wisdom tradition and makes it appear novel, by using it as a cornerstone of his message.

The thesis of the poem is that there is a time for everything, and the thesis is illustrated by a list of opposites. At one level, the poem is simply describing reality as we all know it. In everyone's life there is a time to be born and a time to die, a time to weep and a time to laugh, and so forth. But the poem not only says that things are so. It also affirms that each of these opposites is good and appropriate in its time. There is no such thing as an inherently bad action: there is a time to kill as well as a time to heal, a time to hate as well as a time to love. This idea evidently flies in the face of all moral absolutism. There are no absolutes. Everything is relative to the particular circumstances that surround it. The preacher's task would surely be simplified if Ecclesiastes supplied a list of vices and virtues (as Paul sometimes does) but such lists could only distort the complicated moral issues of life.

Our task is all the more difficult because we have never any guarantee that our timing is in fact right. This does not mean that we never know what is right, only that we have no absolute certainty. Presumably a wise person will fare better than a fool. Ecclesiastes seems to set less store by the ability of the wise than other wisdom books do, but the difference is only one of degree. No wisdom book can claim that the wise are infallible. Much as we might like to proclaim certain truth, the nature of life is such that we must always acknowledge our fallibility.

Ecclesiastes does not suggest that each of the opposites in his list is equally good, and certainly not that each is equally pleasant. He does not describe an ideal universe, but only the world as it is. In fact it is not a view of the world which easily satisfies us. We are left with the question in v. 9: what gain has the worker from his toil? The problem is stated precisely in 3:11: "He has made everything beautiful in its time; also he has put eternity into their minds, except that man can not find out what God has done from the beginning to the end." The word rendered "eternity" here (*olam*) is much disputed. It may refer to the desire for eternal life, or to the *hidden* meaning of life, or the love of the world. In any case, whatever *olam* means, it is frustrated by our inability to find out what God has done. Humanity is not satisfied to be told that everything has its proper time. We want to know how everything fits together, to find some plan and meaning in life. Ecclesiastes does not deny that there may be such a plan, but he evidently does not believe that humanity can know it. No matter how much we toil, the great contradictions of life remain beyond our comprehension.

So while humanity longs to see life as a whole and make clearcut distinctions between right and wrong, we have only a fragmented view in which some things appear better than others at different times. Ecclesiastes accepts this human limitation with a certain resignation. The ultimate questions are God's business. If the world is fragmented, and does not make sense to us, God made it so "in order that men should fear before him" (3:14). Awareness of our ultimate ignorance and dependence is precisely what makes us appreciate our creaturehood and acknowledge a God who is beyond our comprehension. When that acknowledgment has been made, it is possible also to be content with God's gift "that everyone should eat and drink and take pleasure in all his toil" (3:13).

The tone of resignation, and patient acceptance of everything in its time, which dominates this passage, is not very congenial to the taste of modern industrial society. We like to take a more active role, to change what we find unpleasant in life, to persevere in pursuing the problems of life rather than resign ouselves to ignorance. To this mentality Ecclesiastes would surely say: there is a time to change and a time to accept what is given, a time to persevere and a time to give up. Yet, ultimately Ecclesiastes seems to regard all the tremendous human efforts to transform the world as "business that God has given the sons of men to be busy with" (3:10). Is he right? It would surely be a mistake to absolutize the attitude of Ecclesiastes as the right mentality for all occasions. To do so would violate his own basic principle that everything has its time and nothing is absolute. What each preacher must decide is whether the time is ripe for the message of Ecclesiastes. Modern society is heavily achievement-oriented and often takes its labors with ultimate seriousness. Is this precisely the kind of setting where Ecclesiastes needs to be heard? In a fatalistic peasant society, if such is left anywhere, the tone of the book might only depress people to new levels of inactivity. In

the hyperactive society of urban America, however, this counsel of patience and resignation may be precisely the sort of
corrective that we need.

The Common Fate of Beasts and Men (3:16–22)

In 3:16 Ecclesiastes turns to one of the abiding scandals of
life; "in the place of justice, there was wickedness." The following verse cites the standard solution to the problem: "God
will judge the righteous and the wicked." This belief is so
alien to the thought of Ecclesiastes that many commentators
have dismissed it as an editorial gloss. Others assume that Ecclesiastes only cites this view to reject it. The idea of an even-
tual judgment is certainly undermined by the following
verses. The translation of v. 17 is disputed. The Hebrew reads
"for there is a time for every matter and for every work *there.*"
Most commentators (and the RSV) emend the word for
"*there*" and read a verb "he appointed." Some, however suggest that the word "there" is correct and refers to the nether-
world. The sense then would be: if there is a time for
everything, there must be a time for judgment too; however,
that judgment does not seem to come on earth in our life time,
so it must come after we are dead. Since Ecclesiastes shares
the common belief that a person only survives as a shade in
Sheol, without any real vitality, the prospect of a judgment after death provides little consolation. It cannot entail reward
or punishment in any meaningful sense. It certainly does not
remove the scandal of the prosperity of the wicked here and
now.

Whichever interpretation of 3:17 we accept, it is clear
that the idea of a future judgment solves no problems for Ecclesiastes. His sentiments are more truly reflected in vv 18–
21: "the fate of the sons of men and the fate of beasts is the
same; as one dies, so dies the other. They all have the same
breath, and man has no advantage over the beasts; for all is
vanity . . . who knows whether the spirit of man goes upward
and the spirit of the beast goes down to the earth?" The force
of this view lies in the concluding question—who knows what
happens after death? The fact of death is indisputable. Human
beings and animals alike do in fact die. Whatever "advantage" a person may have acquired during life by wealth, reputation or talent is of no avail in the face of death. Now we

might say that our ignorance of what happens after death cuts both ways. Perhaps the spirit of man does go upward. We can certainly hope. But hope is not knowledge, and it provides no certainty. An experiential, natural theology must place greater weight on the knowledge that comes from our experience than on our hopes for what is beyond our experience. Our experience tells us that we die like the beasts and this is the first thing that our theology must reckon with. Beyond this, we may have hope, but ultimately we do not know.

Ecclesiastes' blunt account of what we know and do not know about death is solidly based on the common human experience. But is it relevant to Christian preaching? Is our situation not different in the light of the Christian faith in resurrection? The question here is, at root, whether Christians are exempted from the common human condition, and the answer, of course, is that they are not. In the NT the resurrection can never be taken in isolation from crucifixion and death. Further, we are never given any guarantee of what will happen to us personally after death. Even those texts such as those in the book of Revelation which give general descriptions of resurrection and final judgment must be read as symbolic gropings after a mysterious reality and not as precise factual information about what will actually happen. Ultimately, such matters as resurrection and the fate of humanity after death are in the hands of God. The response of Jesus to the sons of Zebedee in Mark 10 may serve as a paradigm for the Christian preacher; "The cup that I drink you will drink; and with the baptism with which I am baptized you will be baptized; but to sit at my right hand or my left is not mine to grant, but it is for those for whom it has been prepared" (Mark 10:40). In short, we can know in a general way the fate that awaits us in this life (though not, obviously, in detail) but the hereafter we must leave to God.

The value of Ecclesiastes to the Christian preacher lies in the corrective it can supply to some common Christian attitudes. The belief in the resurrection is too often taken as a guarantee of our personal salvation. It is nothing of the sort. Even when we see the hope of eternal salvation as conditional—a reward for the righteous—we are usually assuming that we belong to that group. Again, we have no such guarantee. Further, and most significantly, a too-ready assurance of afterlife can be used as a shield against the full realization of the ignorance and contingency which characterize the mortal human condition. Immortality can be seen too readily as a goal for human achievement and progress towards that goal can become a standard for rating peoples' performance. The pursuit of immortality can then become like any of the other pursuits criticized by Ecclesiastes—an illusion by which we seek to give ourselves status and deny our full dependence as creatures. Ecclesiastes' reminder of the degree to which we share a common nature with animals can serve as a healthy antidote to the facile complacency and smugness that are too often characteristic of Christians.

It is especially important to note that Ecclesiastes' conclusion from all this is neither indifference nor despair. Quite the contrary; "So I saw that there is nothing better than that a man should enjoy his work, for that is his lot." When we accept that we do not know what happens after death and that there is nothing we can do about it anyway, this acceptance should free us up to enjoy life as we find it. If there is no "profit" to be sought either here or hereafter, then we may concentrate on what we find to be good here and now. Is this the attitude of "eat drink and be merry, for tomorrow we die," which Paul so emphatically rejects in 1 Cor 15? If drinking and merriment is pursued as a goal, as if it were something to be achieved, then Ecclesiastes would obviously dismiss it as "chasing after wind." Also there is no suggestion that we can infringe the rights of others for the sake of our own enjoyment. The entire wisdom tradition insisted that the better enjoyment can be found in fellowship with others. Since we always need other people, anyone who tries to take advantage of others is ultimately a fool, since he will make enemies rather than friends. We shall see more of Ecclesiastes' concern for human solidarity in the following chapter. The counsel to eat, drink and be merry does not necessarily imply irresponsibility or any form of wrongdoing. It is rather a matter of accepting the "portion" or "lot" which God has given, for "apart from him who can eat or who can have enjoyment?" (2:25). There is no particular virtue in asceticism or gloominess. The business of life, for Ecclesiastes, is to be lived now, not deferred to an uncertain afterlife which is beyond the horizon of our knowledge.

Human Solidarity (4)

The Scandal of Oppression (4:1–3; 5:8–9)

Ecclesiastes concluded his reflection on the prominence of injustice in the world with a note of resignation. Our attempts to find a rationale for the ways of God and the world are vain. It is better to take life as it comes and admit that we cannot find a satisfactory solution to the problem of theodicy. All we learn from such problems is our own ignorance, that we "are but beasts" (3:18). Twice in the following two chapters he returns to a related problem—the widespread oppression practiced on earth. Again, he can find no satisfactory explanation. In 4:1–3 his reaction is bitter: "I thought the dead who are already dead more fortunate than the living who are still alive; but better than both is he who has not yet been, and has not seen the evil deeds that are done under the sun." As in 2:17 ("I hated life") this verse expresses the author's immediate reaction to an experience, not his final conclusions about life. It is born out of sympathy with the oppressed and his helplessness to do anything about it. We might think it would be better to *try* to do something about it, to light a candle rather than curse the darkness. However, it is often impossible to do anything more than draw attention to oppression. The prophets, to be sure, often promise a coming divine judgment against the oppressors. Visions of future judgment can also cause us to gloss over the enormity of present suffering and to resign ourselves to it for the present. The bitter reaction of Ecclesiastes has at least the merit of focusing our attention squarely on the intolerable nature of oppression. The realization that life is unbearable in some situations can be a powerful stimulus to revolution. Ecclesiastes does not go so far as to counsel rebellion. When all the power is in the hands of the oppressors (4:1) rebellion may be pointless. However, his blunt honesty refuses to provide any justification for oppression (by saying that it is punishment for sin, or that suffering is meritorious). By declaring oppression to be an intolerable evil he clears the way for a realistic reaction to it. (We should note that even in his bitterness Ecclesiastes does not say, as the Greek tragedians did, that "not to be born is the best thing." He says, better is he who has not *yet* been Perhaps in the future things will be better. At least there is hope, while we can look to the future at all.)

The second passage that reflects on oppression is in 5:8. Here the tone is very different: if you see the poor oppressed, do not be amazed, for each official has someone above him. Also, in all, a king is an advantage to a land. It is surprising that many scholars have accused Ecclesiastes of callousness on the basis of this verse, despite his passionate outburst in 4:1 – 3. When the sage says "do not be surprised" he is not condoning oppression. He is merely being realistic. Nothing is gained by a naive assumption that every official is honest or that justice is always done. The more honestly we see reality for what it is, the better hope we have of coping with it. The concluding comment on the king is, again, not a blanket approval for everything the king does. It is rather an attempt to balance the perspective on political structures. It is always tempting for the preacher to resort to strong contrasts. The temptation is always stronger when we are speaking of politics and public affairs, where we like to see either knights in shining armor or total villains. Yet even a villain can on occasion do more good than harm. Many liberal Americans can find no redeeming value in Richard Nixon, but he undoubtedly made a substantial contribution to world peace, among other things. Chicago has long been governed by a political "machine" that is notoriously corrupt. Yet many aspects of the city are managed more efficiently than is the case in other, less "corrupt" cities. Ecclesiastes shares the concern of the entire wisdom tradition for practical effects, not moral ideals. A strong king, with some oppression, might be better for a land than the chaos of anarchy (depending, of course, on the extent of the oppression). This is not to condone any form of oppression, but simply to realize that our options in life are not between the pure good and pure bad but between the relatively better or worse in any particular situation. Any preacher who undertakes to speak on political issues would do well to keep this passage in mind.

The Value of Fellowship (4:4–12)

Oppression is not just a sin against God. More obviously it is a crime of humanity against humanity. In large part it arises from the human desire for achievement. We try to lift ourselves above our fellows, and often push them down in the process. When human worth is measured comparatively, it is inevitable that we try to increase our relative status by humiliating others. So: "all toil and all skill in work come from a man's envy of his neighbor" (4:4). Yet this also is vanity since our superiority is short-lived. Besides, it is folly, since it isolates us from our fellows, although we will eventually need them—"woe to him who is alone when he falls and has not another to lift him up" (4:10). Love of one's neighbor is not ultimately a matter of supernatural law, but of the natural need of humanity. "If two lie together, they are warm; but how can one be warm alone?" (4:11). Human need is deeper than any particular rule of conduct. Even an enlightened self-interest warns against the isolated ego and points in the direction of community. Two will fare better than one and a three-fold cord is not easily broken (4:9,12).

Toil should be directed to building community, not to the achievement of the individual. So "a person who has no one, either son or brother, yet there is no end of all his toil" (4:8) is especially pathetic. ᵍrom Ecclesiastes' perspective anyone who toils to accumulate wealth is striving after wind, since he does not know what will become of it after his death. Someone who can leave it to his family has some gratification. One who has no family has no "profit" at all.

The pathetic character of a person isolated by his own achievement is further illustrated by the case of the old and foolish king (4:13–16). Ecclesiastes takes the hypothetical case (perhaps suggested by the Joseph story) of a man who rises from prison or poverty to become king. Yet what has he accomplished? Even when he is old and foolish he cannot bring himself to take the advice he needs. Presumably it would be beneath his dignity. His exaltation has cut him off from the help he needs, yet the glory of his position will be soon forgotten. Ecclesiastes reflects that a poor but wise youth who still has his prospects before him is in a preferable position.

The moral of these passages is obvious enough. Kings are not the only people who isolate themselves or forget their need for community. It is a common human predicament. The king in 4:13–16 and the person "who has no one" in 4:7–8 are not sinners in the conventional sense of breaking the commandments. But they are fools. They are sinners in the sense that they "miss the mark" of what life is all about. As such they come within the field of concern of any responsible preacher. Passages like these should broaden our view of the range of theology and preaching.

False Ideals of Worship, Wealth and Wisdom (5–6)

The wisdom literature rarely addresses questions of religious observance in the narrow, cultic, sense. Eccles 5:1 – 7 is one of the few exceptions. These verses clearly show that for Ecclesiastes sacrifices and vows were not of prime importance, and were, in fact, rather dangerous. Better not do them at all than do them badly. Specifically the sage warns against being "rash with your mouth"(5:2). God is in heaven, and we are on earth. Yet when we pray we are easily tempted to forget our earthliness, to boast of our achievements like the Pharisee in the parable, or to presume to tell God what to do. It is a fool who prays with many words. God does not need persuasion, and one who undertakes to persuade God, is, to say the least, arrogant. Again, if a vow is promised, it should be performed. We cannot bluff God by declaring our intentions but not following through. (The meaning of v.6 is uncertain. The "messenger" of the RSV translation may be an angel or may be a clerk of the temple.) The danger of cultic ritual is that we can easily slip into thinking that we can please God by words or by going through the motions. We are tempted to try to impress God by the way we express ourselves before him. God, however, does not need to be impressed and can not be so easily fooled. So "it is better to draw near to listen than to offer the sacrifice of fools"(5:1). The statement that God has no pleasure in fools may sound harsh but it should not surprise us. Virtue cannot be divorced from wisdom, nor sin from folly. The wisdom tradition sets no store by a faith that is blind or a naiveté that is self-deluding.

It is worthwhile to note the similarity between this passage in Ecclesiastes and the advice of Jesus on prayer in Matt 6. Those who pray loudly in public already have their reward. We should not "heap up empty phrases as the Gentiles do."Length or volume do not cause prayers to be heard (Matt 6:5– 8). Most importantly, not everyone who says "Lord,

Lord" will enter the kingdom of heaven (Matt 7:21). The pleasure of God cannot be achieved by our efforts in prayer or cult. Jesus, like Ecclesiastes warns against an active, pushy approach to worship. It should not be our objective to promote ourselves or to persuade God to our way of thinking. Rather we should draw near to listen, and try to understand what is given to us.

A passage such as this can be applied very directly in a sermon on prayer. Prayer, whether public or private, offers endless opportunities for self-delusion. We need hardly say that Ecclesiastes would be rather skeptical of the demonstrative, and sometimes theatrical, prayer style of "charismatic" groups. (Even such a spiritual enthusiast as Paul had his reservations in 1 Cor 14.) Even on a more reflective level, the ideal of a "personal relationship" with God or Christ can be illusory, since it builds up our self-esteem in a way that is subject to little verification. To "draw near to listen" is a critical exercise. It tries to see ourselves as others see us rather than to imagine ourselves as we would like to be. The preacher should not encourage mystification in prayer but try to promote a critical self-consciousness.

The Vanity of Riches

The remainder of chap. 5 and all of chap. 6 reflect on the vanity of riches. The patterns are by now familiar. One who loves money will not be satisfied with it. The more we have the more we need (5:10–11). The problem is that the pursuit of wealth, like the pursuit of anything else in life, is really a pursuit of total and permanent satisfaction, the "eternity" envisaged in the human mind according to Eccles 3:11. Neither wealth nor anything else can provide such fulfilment.

The praise of the laborer's sleep in 5:12 does not imply that poverty is better than wealth, but only that wealth does not guarantee happiness, and may on occasion prevent it.

The incidents recounted in 5:13–17 and in 6:1–6 are closely similar. Both concern the acquisition of wealth which the owner never enjoys. The first incident might be viewed as tragic. A man who toiled to leave a fortune for his son lost it in a bad venture and had nothing in the end. There is nothing to suggest that this man did anything morally wrong. Yet at the end he has "vexation and sickness and resentment." The only one who suffers from his mishap is himself (perhaps also his son) and his suffering is due to the way he had set his hopes on his fortune. The sage warns that such hopes have a shakey foundation and can easily lead to disappointment. Even if this man had been successful in his ventures the statement in 5:15 would still be true: "As he came from his mother's womb he shall go again, naked as he came and shall take nothing for his toil, which he may carry away in his hand." Vexation and resentment are the outcome of our attempted achievements. By contrast, contentment is found in enjoying life as it comes. It should be noted that wealth too is a gift to be enjoyed (5:19). The point is that wealth is given for enjoyment, not for hoarding or as a goal to be sought in itself.

The incident in 6:1–6 makes a similar point. A person who has wealth and prosperity but is unable to enjoy them is more wretched than a still-born child. The wretchedness results from frustrated expectation and desire. The frustration is especially acute in the case of the wealthy man whose ambitions seemed within reach of fulfilment. Yet there is often a tension between the acquisitive urge to accumulate wealth and the ability to enjoy. Enjoyment involves some degree of letting go, of being prepared to spend and share. Most importantly, it is not quantifiable. We cannot add up our enjoyment to show that it is greater than that of other people. It provides no basis for competitive boasting. Yet as Ecclesiastes incessantly reminds us, our comparative superiority over others is an illusion that will pass. The real good in life is the enjoyment of the passing moment.

Ecclesiastes definitively rejects the traditional view that fulfilment can be found in a multitude of children or length of days (6:3–6). Here again the objection is to *quantifying*—a hundred children or a thousand years—as if the number were a guarantee of quality. Happiness cannot be guaranteed by numbers of anything, or by anything that we may have to show externally. It depends on the personal involvement and attitude of the individual in each particular situation. There is no ready-made formula by which it can be assured.

This section, again, can be applied quite directly in preaching on attitudes to wealth. As we have mentioned before, wealth is often a delicate subject for a pastor of a rich church, who benefits from the affluence of his audience. Yet it

is especially in such a context that the subject must be addressed. The harsh denunciations of a prophet like Amos or of
the Book of Revelation are not the only models on which the
preacher can draw. Such direct confrontation may often be
counter-productive. Ecclesiastes suggests a different approach—not a direct assault but rather an invitation to reflect, aided by an occasional anecdote. The style is similar to
that of Jesus in the gospels, except that there we find more
anecdotes and fewer reflections, and the effect is all the better.
As Abraham tells the rich Man in Luke 16: 29– 31, the rich are
not usually impressed by what Moses and the prophets, nor
even one risen from the dead, have to say. They may be impressed by a less passionate appeal to their own long-term
self-interest and the practical limitations of what wealth can
provide.

The Futility of Wisdom (6:7– 12)

Ecclesiastes' keen perception of the futility of wealth and
other human achievements has been shared by many philoso-
phers and theologians at various times. In fact, skepticism is a
traditional characteristic of academics. Very often it is associated with a kind of intellectual arrogance. The skeptic stands
aloof from the follies of mankind. The very wisdom which en-
ables him to see human achievements as folly puts him on
something of a pedestal. It matters little whether that wisdom
is attributed to philosophical insight or to supernatural grace.
In either case wisdom becomes an exception to the vanities of
life and is regarded as a superior state.

Ecclesiastes makes no such claim for wisdom; "What advantage has the wise man over the fool?" Philosophical and
theological treatises do not change the basic conditions of life:
"The more words, the more vanity, and what is man the better?" (6:11). The sight of the eyes is better than the wandering
of desire, but not if we set it up as an ideal to be pursued. Wisdom provides no salvation from the constant flux of time and
the inevitability of death. Therefore it should not be taken too
seriously. It does not after all come to grips with the most basic human problems.

Why then did Ecclesiastes bother to write his book? Wisdom is no more permanent a prize than any other, but at least
it has a negative function. It can open our eyes to the vanity of

all pursuits. It can disabuse us of the illusionary achievements
and "profits" on which we pin our hopes. In so doing, wisdom
can free us from false objectives in life and give us the liberty
to enjoy the life that is given to us.

These reflections are instructive for the light they shed on
what any preacher or teacher may hope to achieve. Definitive
answers to the problems of life are usually beyond us, but we
can at least expose false answers and come to a realistic appraisal of the problems.

The Relativity of Wisdom and Righteousness (7)

The Ambiguity of Wisdom (7:1–14)

The concluding verses of chap. 6 (6:7– 12) mark a point of
transition in Ecclesiastes. The skeptical view of wisdom in
these verses might be considered an appropriate conclusion to
chapters 1– 6, or equally, as an introduction to chapters 7–
12. Some scholars make the break at 6:10 and regard 6:10– 12
as a keynote for the following chapters.

The second half of the book has proved far more difficult
for interpreters than the first. Many passages (e.g. 8:10– 17)
are written in the familiar style of Ecclesiastes, as reflections
on the sages' own experience. Other passages, however, look
like collections of traditional proverbs (e.g. 7: 1– 12). The
problem for the interpreter is especially related to these traditional passages. Do they represent the views of Ecclesiastes, or
does he only cite them to refute them by his more personal reflections? Distinguished scholars have defended each of these
ways of interpreting Ecclesiastes. The preacher who is not a
professional scholar may be readily forgiven if he or she is a
little confused.

At the outset, it is well to bear in mind two fundamental
principles which should be clear by now. First, even traditional wisdom, as we found it in the book of Proverbs, does not
claim to provide clearcut, right or wrong, answers to the
problems of life. We saw in Prov 26 for example, that contradictory proverbs could be placed side by side, without any explanation. One may apply in one situation; its opposite in
another. Wisdom is not simply a matter of knowing the right
answers, but of having the *timing* to know when an answer
fits. This characteristic of all proverbial wisdom is especially

prominent in Ecclesiastes—as we have seen above in connection with Eccles 3:1 – 15. Accordingly, if we find contradictory opinions in Ecclesiastes, we should not be too hasty to assume that he agrees with one and rejects the other. A second principle follows from this. One of the basic tenets of Ecclesiastes is that there are no absolute answers. When we read a statement (e.g. "sorrow is better than laughter") we like to think that it is either true or false. Now for Ecclesiastes, any statement that is taken absolutely is vanity, since there are bound to be exceptions. He refuses to gratify our desire for absolute statements. It is no accident then that interpreters have been perplexed as to which of the opinions found in these chapters truly represent the views of the author. Our perplexity arises from our desire for clarity. The apparent confusion in Ecclesiastes accurately represents the author's viewpoint. All "wisdom" can give us is a series of insights that are partially true. If we try to absolutize any of them we are chasing an illusion of absolute truth, and that, of course, is "vanity."

In the light of these remarks we now turn to 7: 1 – 14. Vv. 1 – 6 consist in large part of a series of sayings that one thing is better than another. The tone of these sayings is gloomy, to say the least. The day of death is better than the day of birth, sorrow is better than mirth, the rebuke of the wise than the song of fools. Then in v. 6, after the laughter of fools is compared to the crackling of thorns under a pot, the sage adds "this too is vanity." We are left to decide whether his judgment applies only to the laughter of fools or to the entire series of sayings that has gone before. On the one hand the gloomy tone of these sayings is typical enough of Ecclesiastes. On the other hand, they do not fit well with his counsel to enjoy life as it comes. In 7:14 this section concludes with the advice to be joyful in the day of prosperity. Should we conclude then that Ecclesiastes simply rejects the opinions of 7:1 – 6? Not quite. I would suggest that the judgment "this too is vanity" does indeed apply to all the preceding verses. But "vanity" is not quite the same as "wrong." What he means is that these verses cannot be taken as absolutes. They are vapor: they fit one situation but then they fade away. The pursuit of gloominess is no more satisfactory than the pursuits of wealth, pleasure or wisdom. Yet these sayings are not simply wrong. They too have their proper time. The harshest of them is probably the second

part of 7:1: the day of death is better than the day of birth. It
has been suggested that this statement must be read in the
light of the preceding line: a good name is better than precious ointment. The test of a good name is how it holds up on
the day of death. So the final assessment at death is more significant than the facile expectations and promises at birth.
This is at least one possible respect in which the day of death
is "better" than the day of birth, but this is not the only way in
which the verse may be un erstood. Death may appear preferable for various reasons at various times. A similar point is
made in 7:8. "Better is the end of a thing than the beginning,
and the patient in spirit is better than the proud in spirit." The
point here is that it is better to have the patience to wait and
see how something will work out, than to presume success in
advance. It is more satisfactory to be successful at the end
than to ride high in expectation and then be disappointed. The
effect of this saying is to warn us of the variability of fortune,
and so of the danger of hasty conclusions. A saying like this
has a peculiarly self-negating effect. Since we cannot predict
the "end of a thing" we cannot even be certain that patience is
the best policy. We have no certainty, and it would be vanity
to claim that we have. All the advice of the sage stands under
this qualification. It may be the best we can do, but we should
not take it for an absolute revelation.

The other sayings in 7:7 – 14 further qualify the claims of
wisdom. Over against the sayings that sorrow is better than
laughter (7:1 – 6) is set the reminder that oppression makes
the wise foolish (7:7). Sorrow and affliction can have destructive effects, just as poverty is no more a virtue in itself than
wealth. Circumstances may incline a person to take bribes,
and distort his idea of wisdom.

Vv. 11 – 12 make an interesting comparison between wisdom and money. Both are useful, if they are put to use to pro-
tect the life of one who has them. Both are for the service of
life. Neither is an end in itself.

Wisdom too cannot be made the basis of comparisons.
The contrast of the present with former times does not arise
from wisdom (7:10). Wisdom rather demands that one take
the present as it comes, and not attempt to grade it relative to
other times.

The conclusion of the section in 7:13 – 14 repeats the familiar message of Ecclesiastes. What is crooked cannot be made straight (compare 1:15). Here he adds the thought that crooked and straight are both the work of God. Nothing is gained by pursuing theodicy. We cannot explain the ways of God, or why the world is as it is. V. 14 suggests that God made the world confusing so that humanity would realize its own ignorance and be content to enjoy the world as it comes, and not "play God" by trying to explain it. Any preacher would do well to bear this in mind.

Do Not Be Too Righteous (7:15–20)

The following section pushes the relativizing tendency of Ecclesiastes to an extreme. First, he claims "to have seen it all"—every possible variation is encountered in experience. You may find a righteous person who perishes and a sinner who prospers—no matter what traditional dogma says. So the sage reaches the startling conclusion: "Be not righteous overmuch, and do not make yourself overwise; why should you destroy yourself." Some scholars have regarded this verse as the very heart of Ecclesiastes' advice. Others regard it as an opinion which he implicitly rejects. Now it is true that all the sage's advice is to some degree qualified. The whole point of a saying like this is that one should not try to be perfect—and so one should not think that one can be perfect by following this particular maxim. Ecclesiastes is not giving a key to perfection. He is insisting that there is no such key. Granted that qualification, however, this saying is quite typical of Ecclesiastes and there is nothing to suggest that he rejects it. (Such counsels of moderation are also typical of much ancient wisdom—remember the famous maxim of the Delphic oracle "nothing too much"). The shocking aspect, from the perspective of the preacher, is the suggestion that to be over righteous is a bad thing. Is it possible to be over-righteous? One thinks of the Pharisee and the Publican, although we may wish to deny that the Pharisee was *truly* righteous. However, the point in Ecclesiastes is that any *pursuit* is a bad thing. What is true of the pursuit of wealth or wisdom is no less true of the pursuit of righteousness. When an individual sets out to excel in righteousness or even securely to establish himself as righteous, then righteousness becomes a "profit" or "gain" and, like all human achievements, mere vanity. We may compare St.

Paul's polemic against "righteousness by works" but we should also be aware that "faith" too can often function just like works. Even if one regards righteousness as a gift of grace, and not as a human achievement, there may still be a problem. What matters is how we conceive of the end result. If we think that we are or can become righteous and enjoy righteousness as a state, then righteousness becomes an "immortality symbol," something secure and permanent which lifts us out of the vapor of all things human. Whether this state is a result of works, faith or grace matters little. It lifts us out from the common herd and gives us a "profit" in life. But, says Ecclesiastes, such "profit" is an illusion. No one is actually freed from the ambiguity of the common human condition so as to be absolutely "righteous." "Surely there is not a righteous man on earth who does good and never sins" (7:20). Righteous and sinner are never absolute categories. We should not listen to hear whether others curse us— for we know that we have cursed others. Such is the human condition and it cannot be escaped. The preacher of wisdom urges us to accept that reality and face up to it, not to deny it by attempting to be "over-righteous." The pursuit of righteousness, even the conception of righteousness as an absolute state, inevitably leads to illusion.

This passage can serve as a useful corrective to the usual tendency of preachers to present absolute ideals. In fact, it is very difficult to preach without seeming to absolutize the good we perceive at the moment. How can this be avoided? Ecclesiastes tries to look at particular incidents from experience so that the limitations of each situation make it difficult to generalize. This technique is more clearly developed in the parables of Jesus. A story like the Good Samaritan illustrates what righteousness involves in a particular case, but the case is particular. Different circumstances might call for a different response. Ideals are always abstract. A preacher is better advised to deal with concrete instances where the implications of the ideal can be clearly perceived.

Can We Attain Wisdom (7:23–8:1)

There is a similar problem with the pursuit of wisdom. The traditional praises of the wise man (e.g. 7:19;8:1) may be true enough, but when we pursue wisdom in its absolute form we must admit with the sage, that we fall far short of it. If there is such a thing as complete wisdom, if there is a "sum of things" (7:25) no human can know it. The conclusions of human wisdom are relative at best.

The particular example of the relativity of wisdom in 7:26 – 28 concerns the traditional evaluation of women. Very often in antiquity woman was viewed as the temptress (cf. Prov 5 – 9). Ecclesiastes shares this view, somewhat chauvinistically perhaps. Yet he puts it in perspective: "One man among a thousand I found, but a woman among all these I have not found" (7:28). (Presumably he means "good" men and women. We are reminded of the Greek Cynic philosopher who walked about with a candle in the marketplace looking for "a man.") He confirms the traditional negative judgment on women, but men are little better. One should not think, then, that all the woes of humanity can be blamed on women. A simple distinction between good and wicked cannot be made on the basis of sex, or, indeed on any other basis either.

Fate and Free Will (7:29)

The concluding verse of chap. 7 is significant. Elsewhere Ecclesiastes frequently insists that the world is as God made it and cannot be changed. As he asks in 7:13: "who can make straight what he (God) has made crooked." In 7:29, however, he asserts that God made man "straight" (*yashar*, "straight or upright"). Corruption is due to the devices of humanity. This verse should warn us against assuming that Ecclesiastes was a fatalist. In fact the book has no clear discussion of fate and free will. The sage clearly realized the limitations of what humanity can control. Yet he does not deny human responsibility for "crookedness." Our responsibility may be relative, given our ignorance and the inclinations we are born with, but it is still real. The deviousness of human ways is an obvious fact of experience, and this is the only explanation for sin that interests Ecclesiastes. After all, it is the only one we can do anything about.

Attitudes to Secular Authority (8:2 – 5)

Much of the time Ecclesiastes is concerned with those things about which we cannot do anything. The power of the king often fell into this category, at least as far as most people were concerned. The advice to obey the king's command in Eccles 8 is less a matter of virtue than of practical necessity. Nevertheless 8:5 must give us pause: "He who obeys a command will meet no harm, and the wise man will know the time and way." There can be little doubt that the command in question is the king's command. (Some commentators take it as the Law of Moses, which is conspicuously absent in Ecclesiastes.) We touch here on one of the weak points of the wisdom literature. It has a definite tendency to conform to the status quo. We miss the impassioned rhetoric of the prophets, who were willing to challenge the royal command on occasion. Yet we should not assume that this conformism was peculiar to the wisdom literature. St. Paul was much more emphatic in the letter to the Romans: "Let every person be subject to the governing authorities. For there is no authority except from God and those that exist have been instituted by God. Therefore he who resists the authorities resists what God has appointed..." (Rom 13: 1–2).

In the light of the Pauline statement, if not of Ecclesiastes, is the Christian preacher obliged to support the status quo and teach that obedience is a virtue? Such a view has always had wide support in Christianity, but it is by no means necessary. There are plenty of biblical precedents, from the OT prophets to the Apocalypse of John, for criticism of secular authority. Within the context of a wisdom theology, we must continually test the formulations of tradition against our own experience. After Nuremberg and Watergate it is no longer possible for us to accept Ecclesiastes' saying that "he who obeys a command will meet no harm." If we follow the sage's own fidelity to experience, we must say that his conclusion on this point is no longer satisfactory.

Yet we should note a difference between the attitudes of Ecclesiastes and Paul. Ecclesiastes does not regard obedience to the king as a virtue, but as a tactic of self-preservation. The further remark, that the mind of a wise man will know the time and the way, even suggests that one may use discretion to avoid any actual wrongdoing while still appearing to obey. This latter suggestion may also be somewhat offensive to modern morality. We often place great value on speaking our mind openly and publicly. Biblical wisdom, by contrast, is less concerned with the individual's feeling of authenticity and honesty than with practical effects. There is no inherent virtue in incurring the wrath of a king (or a policeman). It is often better to avoid confrontation and work quietly behind the scenes. The merit of the discreet way of Ecclesiastes will vary from one situation to another. Sometimes confrontation may be necessary. However, in a generation still marked by the conflicts and memories of the Vietnam era, it is well to consider whether confrontation is not sometimes counter-productive and whether total public honesty is alway either necessary or beneficial.

Life Without Retribution (8:6–17)

The remainder of chap. 8 deals with the problem of justice and injustice. While one man has power over another for harm (8:9), no one has power over the day of death (8:8). Everything has its proper time (8:6) but the sentence against evil deeds does not come speedily (8:11). In 8:12 – 13 Ecclesiastes appears to be reciting a traditional belief "yet I know that it will be well with those who fear God. . ."—a sentiment foreign to the general thought of Ecclesiastes. The Anchor Bible translation accurately captures the meaning of this verse: "I am aware [of what is said,] that "it will be well [in the end] with those who reverence God . . ." The sage is showing his familiarity with the traditional dogma, but the evidence available to him runs contrary to the tradition. Righteous people seem to get what the wicked should get, and vice versa (8:14). Ecclesiastes does not conclude that wickedness is profitable. Wickedness will not "deliver those who are given to it" (8:8) and is of no more advantage in the day of death than any other pursuit. Instead he repeats his familiar message of enjoyment (8:15). This message is reinforced by our inability to find any "profitable" pursuit in life or even to understand "the work that is done under the sun." There is no point to toiling to understand the world. Even the wise man who claims to know cannot in fact find the answers (8:17). The best thing to do, then is not to toil for any illusionary goal, but to enjoy life as best we can.

The blunt honesty of Ecclesiastes in this passage is an important corrective to the pious platitudes about retribution which we found even in the canonical book of proverbs on a few occasions.

Life in the Shadow of Death (9:1–16)

The rationale for Ecclesiastes' counsel of enjoyment is more fully set forth in chap. 9. The ultimate test which shows the futility of human achievements is the inevitability of death. Death is the great leveller. It respects neither the righteous nor the wicked, and does not ask whether one practiced sacrifice or not. From one perspective, indeed this is "an evil in all that is done under the sun"(9:3) since it frustrates our natural ambitions and our desire for retribution. But death also defines the limits of the human condition, within which fulfilment must be found. It is the guarantor of ultimate human equality. In frustrating our attempts to rise above the common condition it throws us back to the solidarity of a humanity that shares the same fate. Death does not deprive life of all value. A living dog is still better than a dead lion—not because it has any ultimate "gain," but because it has the present power to enjoy. Only the living can experience and enjoy. Conversely, life is given to be enjoyed. The statement that "God has already approved what you do" (9:7) is not, of course, a blanket approval of anything a person may do, but refers to eating bread with enjoyment and drinking wine with a merry heart. The point is that God does not require us to be ascetic. If he gives us the chance to enjoy ourselves, we should take it. We may compare the response of Jesus in John 12, when Judas complained that the precious ointment should be sold and the money given to the poor. The poor are always with us (and should certainly not be neglected) but opportunities for enjoyment are rare enough in life that we should take them when they come. It is of course understood that our enjoyment should not infringe on the rights of others. The advice of the sage reflects the normal human way: "enjoy life with the wife whom you love..." (9:9).

Ecclesiastes 9 has often been aptly compared with a passage in the old Babylonian version of the Gilgamesh epic, from the early second millennium B.C. There an "alewife" discourages Gilgamesh from his pursuit of immortality:

> Gilgamesh, whither rovest thou?
> The life thou pursuest thou shalt not find.
> When the gods created mankind
> Death for mankind they set aside,

Life in their own hands retaining.
Thou, Gilgamesh, let full be thy belly.
Make thou merry by day and by night.
Of each day make thou a feast of rejoicing,
Day and night dance thou and play!
Let thy garments be sparkling fresh,
Thy head be washed; bathe thou in water.
Pay heed to the little one that holds on to thy hand,
Let thy spouse delight in thy bosom!
For this is the task of [mankind]!

The story of Adam and Eve in Genesis, where humanity is barred from the "tree of life," makes essentially a similar point. We need not assume that Ecclesiastes was influenced by either Gilgamesh or Genesis. The ideas involved are part of the common wisdom of the ancient Near East. They require no special revelation, but they are deeply rooted in the common human heritage. In each case the inevitability of death sets the boundaries within which positive human fulfilment is possible. The key to happiness lies in the realization of one's proper "portion" in life and refraining from the vain pursuit of something more.

Two further passages in chap. 9 elaborate the basic themes of the chapter. First, in 9: 11– 12, the race is not to the swift nor the battle to the strong. So neither speed nor strength nor anything else that we might pursue and cultivate can guarantee success. Time and chance show that all such pursuits are vapor, but they also show the basic equality of all humanity, which no one can escape.

The second passage, in 9:13– 16, illustrates the frustration of wisdom. A poor wise man saved his city. Yet it brought him no honor or reward. Wisdom is still better than might, in the view of the sage, not because of any profit but because of its inherent enjoyment.

Eccl 9 raises again for the Christian preacher the problem of how this emphasis on death should be related to the Christian teaching on resurrection. We have already discussed this problem with reference to chap. 3, so a few brief remarks may suffice here. The purpose of Ecclesiastes' emphasis on death is to deflate the claims and achievements of humanity, and remind us of our contingency and dependence as creatures. The belief in immortality can easily be used as a cushion to assure us that all is not, after all, vapor. It can give us a sense of permanence and security that lessens our consciousness of creaturehood. The Christian teaching on resurrection was never intended to shield us from the reality of death or to give us security before God. Ecclesiastes can serve as a healthy corrective to a complacent idea of immortality and reinforce the basic Christian (and Jewish) idea of creaturehood. Further, in the last analysis, no one knows what happens after death (and Ecclesiastes might add "even though a wise man claims to know, he cannot find it out" (8:17). The focus of Christian life is not on the hereafter, which is not within our reach, but on the present, for which we are responsible. In the words of the Sermon on the Mount: "Do not be anxious for tomorrow, for tomorrow will be anxious for itself. Let the day's own trouble be sufficient for the day" (Matt 6:34). Ecclesiastes' emphasis on death, time and chance serves to show the futility of human anxiety. The message of Jesus in Matt 6 is in many respects similar. No one can add to his stature by anxiety, either in this life or the next. It is necessary to refrain from the pursuits of anxiety if we are to be free to appreciate the life that is given to us in the present.

Coping with Uncertainty (9:17– 11:7)

Chap. 10 is perhaps the most frustrating chapter of Ecclesiastes for the interpreter. It is made up largely of independent proverbs, many of which seem to be traditional sayings, and it is difficult to judge how far Ecclesiastes endorses them. As in chap. 7, frustration may be the appropriate reaction, and precisely what the sage intended to convey. The traditional sayings are not simply rejected. All have some grain of truth in them. But then, like all proverbs, they admit of so many exceptions! So, wisdom is better than weapons of war, but what good is that when one fool can undo what the wise have accomplished, just as a dead fly can spoil a box of ointment? Wisdom provides seasoned advice for dealing with rulers, but what good is it, if the ruler himself is a fool? (10:5 – 7). Wisdom helps one to succeed, but what good is knowing how to charm a snake if it bites before it is charmed? (10:11). Even the routine tasks of life, like digging a hole or splitting logs, can go wrong and prove dangerous.

What is one to conclude from all this? We might expect

that such an acute awareness of the uncertainties of life would paralyze the sage into complete inactivity, but this is not the case. Instead he finds it chastening and becomes all the more realistic. We should not claim too much certainty or expect too much. One who "multiplies words though no man knows what is to be" is a fool. Also, one who toils without knowing what he can achieve is a fool, and will only fatigue himself (10:14– 15). More positively, there are certain ground rules which one can follow. They certainly do not guarantee success, but they improve one's chances. Drunkenness and sloth should be avoided, and one should not curse the king. The traditional proverb that "money answers everything" (10:19) is relativized by its context here. Money does not solve all problems, but it often helps.

Ecclesiastes' advice for coping with the uncertainties of life is most clearly formulated in 11: 1– 6. We cannot live life if we become obsessed with the uncertainties: "He who observes the wind will not sow; and he who regards the clouds will not reap" (11:4). We must get on with the business of living, but we must do so in such a way that takes account of the uncertainties. "In the morning sow your seed, and at evening withhold not your hand, for you do not know which will prosper, this or that, or whether both alike will be good" (11:6). It is necessary to take risks: "Cast your bread upon the waters for you will find it after many days. Give a portion to seven or even to eight, for you know not what evil may happen on earth" (11:1– 2). Traditionally these sayings have been thought to recommend charity. More recent commentators take them as practical business advice. So the NEB translates: "Send your grain across the seas, and in time you will get a return. Divide your merchandise among seven ventures, eight maybe. . ." In either case the logic is the same. If these verses do indeed recommend charity, it is with an eye to self-interest. We may compare the gospel advice to make friends with the "mammon of iniquity" for we never know when we may need them. The consequence, then, of the uncertainty of life is that we have to hedge our bets. We cannot afford to relax and take things for granted, but also we cannot afford to be arrogant, too sure that our way is right or that we do not need others. The ethic that emerges is a cautious one, but also a modest one that acknowledges and respects our limitations.

This section can scarcely be said to offer exciting possibilities to the preacher. But then, excitement is never the goal of wisdom. The sage's awareness of the uncertainty and ambiguity of life does not make it easy to produce impassioned rhetoric of commitment to a cause. It militates against the clearcut distinctions of right and wrong that might arouse the emotions of a congregation. The balanced reflection on various possibilities can easily become monotonous and boring. It calls for humor and for illustration with concrete examples—more than is provided by the sequence of proverbs in Eccl 10. (Several of the individual sayings—e.g. 10:8–11— could be developed into amusing anecdotes. Proverbs are often compressed outlines for stories or parables.) Yet the challenge of preaching such a view of life is clearly worthwhile if we want a faith that is grounded in understanding rather than a blind faith that is swayed by prejudice.

The Prospect of Aging and Death (11:8–10)

The concluding verses of chapter 11 mark the transition from the reflection on the uncertainties of life to the allegory of old age in chap. 12. Amid all the variables of life one thing is certain—the prospect of death. This prospect sharpens the imperative to enjoy life while it lasts. The knowledge that "the days of darkness will be many" makes the days of light all the more precious. Yet Ecclesiastes does not recommend irresponsible enjoyment: "but know that for all these things God will bring you into judgment" (11:9). The idea of a divine judgment plays little part in Ecclesiastes, and a judgment after death would be very difficult to reconcile with his beliefs. Accordingly, many commentators think that this statement was inserted by an editor, to make the book more orthodox. It is possible, however, that the verse comes from Ecclesiastes. It does not make clear how God will bring one into judgment. It simply asserts that there is a God and that we are responsible for what we do. The judgment of God might work itself out in the "natural" consequences of our action. The important point is that we do not control the consequences of our actions. We cannot simply do what we like and be sure that we will attain the results we want. The dependent character of the human condition requires that we respect the forces of life that are beyond our control. This is essentially what is meant throughout the wisdom tradition by the "fear of the Lord," and it is thoroughly compatible with the thought of Ecclesiastes.

The reference to divine judgment should not be read only as a warning against transgression by enjoying oneself at the expense of others. It also reinforces the imperative that life is to be enjoyed. To fail to appreciate the possibilities for joy in life is to "miss the mark" or sin, and for that too God will bring us into judgment.

The Allegory of Old Age (12:1– 8)

The book of Ecclesiastes concludes with a poetic allegory of old age in 12:1– 8. (12:9– 14 is an epilogue added by later editors.) This poem balances the opening poem in 1:1– 11 and shares the same theme—all is vanity or vapor. 12:1– 8 has been very widely recognized as an allegory of old age, but there is no agreement on how the details should be interpreted. Some commentators have attempted to see each phrase as a description of the failure of some bodily organ. So in 12:3 the "keepers of the house" and the "strong men" might refer to the arms and legs, the grinders to the teeth and "those that look through the windows" as the eyes. The almond tree that blossoms in 12:5 might also refer to the greying of the hair, but the other details of the poem do not suggest such ready allegories for the body. Other commentators take the passage as an account of a storm, night-fall or the ruin of an estate, any of which could serve as a metaphor for old age. It seems better to recognize that the passage does not develop a single image but places together a number of different figures each of which suggests decay and disintegration. The power of the passage does not rest in the identification of each item but in the cumulative impression of collapse, culminating in the conclusion that all things pass, all is vapor.

The opening verse (12:1) clearly shows that the passage as a whole is intended as an allegory for old age and death, when "the evil days come, and the years draw nigh when you will say, 'I have no pleasure in them.'" (Not every detail of an allegory has to correspond directly to something else. It is sufficient that the general impression correspond to the subject that is being described.) 12:1 also gives the main purpose for the reflection on the vapor of life: "Remember your creator in

the days of your youth." The word for "creator" is slightly
problematic, since it is in the plural in Hebrew (bor'eka). Also
the Hebrew word is very similar to the word for "pit" or
"grave" (bor) and to the word for "well" or "source" (be'er).
The Anchor Bible emends the text here to read "grave" (bor).
There is a rabbinic saying, attributed to Rabbi Akiba, that one
should "know whence you came (your source) whither you are
going (your grave) and before whom you are destined to give
an accounting (your creator)." From the perspective of Ecclesiastes, the three ideas are closely related. Birth and death are
the great boundaries of human life that most clearly show our
dependence on the greater power of the Creator. To remember
either one's source or one's grave is to remember that one is a
creature. This acknowledgment goes hand in hand with the
realization that all is "vapor," that everything in life passes
and nothing is permanent or self-sufficient. This perspective
on the world is the basis for the fear of the Lord, which, in the
formulation of Proverbs, is the beginning of wisdom and is also the key to contentment.

It is certainly not surprising that Ecclesiastes should conclude his book with a reflection on old age and death. But why
should he speak metaphorically of a time when "the sun and
moon are darkened and the clouds return after the rain" and
so forth? We have seen a little in the book of Proverbs of the
uses of allegory. One suggestion is that it gives us a fresh new
way of looking at something that has become too familiar. The
somewhat mysterious references to the silver cord and the
golden bowl (12:6) intrigue us and hold our attention better
than a routine, literal description of the symptoms of old age.
More significantly for our purpose, the allegory enlarges our
view of the subject. Eccl 12:1 – 6 suggests not only the decline
of the individual in old age, but even the end of the world,
with the failure of the sun and moon and cosmic light. What
we get from this passage is the sense of an ending, whether of
an individual or an estate or civilization, or the world itself. It
is interesting to compare the images of Ecclesiastes with an
account of the end of the world in one of the great Jewish
apocalypses, Syriac or Second Baruch, written about A.D.
100: "For the youth of the world is passed and the strength of
the creation is already exhausted. . .and the pitcher is near to
the cistern, and the ship to the port, and the course of the jour-

ney to the city and life to (its) consummation" (2 Baruch 85:10).

Ecclesiastes did not in fact expect the end of the world (Eccl. 1:4: "A generation comes and a generation goes but the earth remains forever"). Any suggestion of cosmic collapse in 12:1–6 must be taken as a figurative, poetic projection of the human fate onto the universe. Eschatology, in the sense of matters relating to the end of the world or the messianic age has no place in either Proverbs or Ecclesiastes. Yet the conclusion of Ecclesiastes can be called eschatological in the sense that it proclaims an *end* to *our* world. Just as Amos proclaimed an end to the world of Israel, without implying that the physical world would end, so Ecclesiastes proclaims an *end* to every individual life and indeed to everything in this world which is subject to change. While the apocalyptic writers preached that the present world is passing away, to be replaced by a new one, Ecclesiastes teaches, more radically, that *all* is passing vapor. The present world order is indeed passing away, but the new age that follows it will pass too.

The eschatological tone of this concluding passage of Ecclesiastes can provide a perspective on proverbial wisdom as a whole. Wisdom often gives the impression of a static world view, geared to accepting the status quo. Yet we have seen repeatedly (e.g. Prov. 27, Eccl 3) that proverbial wisdom is founded on a lively sense of the *temporality* of existence, a sense that circumstances are constantly changing, so that there are no fixed absolutes. The consciousness that everything passes away is especially obvious in Ecclesiastes. This sense of the constant flux of time undermines any impression that the world is static. No status quo will remain forever. From this perspective there is always hope for political change and there is also the assurance that no structures, no matter how powerful, will last forever. In general, both Proverbs and Ecclesiastes are more concerned to cope realistically with the powers that be in the present, than with predicting their overthrow. Yet the shadow of decline and death that puts all creation in perspective for Ecclesiastes hangs over the powerful as well as over the oppressed. The sages do not promise that changes will necessarily be for the better, and do not indulge in revolutionary rhetoric about coming utopias. But then, what revolution ever has produced a utopia? Eccle-

siastes' sense of the transience of all things allows us to hope
for improvement but it is too realistic to promise us a messianic age. In this respect every preacher has something to learn
from Ecclesiastes. There is certainly a time for preaching utopias and for dreaming ideals. But there is also always a need
to criticize dreams and to know their limitations. It is also important to be aware that human hopes are not ultimately
grounded in any promise of utopia but in the more ambiguous
reality of ongoing change.

The conclusion of Ecclesiastes can also be instructive for
the modern preacher in suggesting a perspective on the eschatological prophecies in other biblical books. We know that the
earliest Christians fully expected the return of the Lord and
the dissolution of the world within a generation (see e.g. 1
Thess. 4– 5). We also know that this did not happen. Further,
no one who is at all familiar with the history of millennarian
movements through the centuries can set much faith in the
predictions of fundamentalist evangelicals that the book of
Revelation and other prophecies will be fulfilled in our own
time. Such predictions have proven wrong far too often already. However, the preacher who cannot take eschatological
prophecy seriously as prediction may be embarrassed as to
what to do with it. Should it be dismissed as simply errone-
ous? The conclusion of Ecclesiastes may provide a helpful perspective here. The world itself may not be coming to an end,
but the world as we know it is constantly passing away. Also
the various "worlds" of politics, economics and even religion
are never permanent, but, as Ecclesiastes would say, are vapor. Eschatological prophecy is always relevant to this temporal aspect of the reality we live in. The allegorical passage
in Ecclesiastes 12 can suggest a way in which language that
alludes to the end of the world can be used to express the transience of the human condition.

The Epilogue (12:9– 13)

The book in its present form concludes with three editorial reflections. The first (12:9– 10) simply comments on the effort that Ecclesiastes expended on his work. That should be
obvious enough. The "vanity" of all things did not lead him to
the conclusion that nothing mattered, or deserved effort. It is
perhaps significant that the sage's proper name is not known.

His effort was not directed to making his name famous, but to increasing understanding.

The remaining two reflections stand in sharp contrast to the spirit of the book. Vv. 11 – 12 declare that the collected sayings are "firmly planted nails" and warn us to "beware of anything beyond these." We heartily agree with the comment that "of making many books there is no end, and much study is a weariness of the flesh" but we cannot solve our problems by taking a closed canon and avoiding anything outside it. The canon of scripture is essentially a collection of the literature that grew out of the Israelite and early Christian tradition. Such a collection served the purpose of any anthology. It brought together the most important texts in a convenient and manageable way and provided a sort of reference library of the basic works. However, the tradition did not stop when the collection was made, and the experience of subsequent generations did not become less important. The canon should serve to preserve the more ancient works and keep them in circulation, but not to suppress new reflections. Evidently, Ecclesiastes himself did not regard the tradition he received as a finished product, but saw fit to criticize and expand it from his own experience. If we are faithful to the spirit of Ecclesiastes we in turn cannot accept his findings as final but must test them in the light of ongoing experience, even if that involves study and a weariness of the flesh.

The final reflections have a similar restrictive tone: "Fear God and keep his commandments; for this is the whole duty of man" (12:13). We found no clear reference in Ecclesiastes itself to the commandments of God or the specific Mosaic law. The sage would surely have agreed that it is better to keep those commandments, but it is doubtful whether he would have equated the fear of the Lord so simply with keeping the Law. The whole duty of man, for Ecclesiastes was not only to keep specific commandments. It involved the enjoyment of life and the appreciation of the variety of situations in which we find ourselves. More fundamentally the "whole duty of man" sounds like a foolproof recipe for ultimate success. While the Law, as St. Paul would say, is holy and just and good, it does not in itself assure success or salvation. Ecclesiastes knew as well as Paul that we cannot attain an ultimate "profit" or salvation by "the works of the Law." Life cannot be reduced to such a formula. The pursuit of the Law, like any other pursuit that is thought to ensure salvation or "profit", would be considered by Ecclesiastes as "vanity" or chasing after wind.

The editorial additions, then, seem to miss the point of Ecclesiastes and speak from a very different viewpoint. Such contrasting viewpoints are not unusual in scripture. A sensitive reader quickly learns that the Bible does not provide a set of consistent answers. In many cases the diverse viewpoints may complement each other, just as contradictory proverbs may be valid in different situations. In other cases we may have to choose between viewpoints that are genuinely incompatible. From the perspective of the natural theology of the wisdom literature all tradition, including scripture, must be tried and tested in the light of our experience. We cannot in conscience preach a traditional dogma (e.g. that the righteous always prosper) if it falsifies our own experience. Not least of the lessons of Ecclesiastes is the critical attitude to tradition and scripture which refuses to accept them as fixed dogmas but is prepared to wrestle with them for insights that can inform our lives.

Bibliography

The best and most thorough study of the OT wisdom literature is that of Gerhard von Rad, *Wisdom in Israel* (Nashville: Abingdon, 1972). This can be supplemented by the fine collection of scholarly essays in J. L. Crenshaw, ed. *Studies in Ancient Israelite Wisdom* (New York: Ktav, 1976). Less detailed, but still scholarly treatments of the wisdom literature can be found in O. S. Rankin, *Israel's Wisdom Literature* (New York: Schocken, 1969, first published, 1936), R. B. Y. Scott, *The Way of Wisdom* (New York: Macmillan, 1971) and J.M. Thompson, *The Form and Function of Proverbs in Ancient Israel* (The Hague: Mouton, 1974). A good introduction from a pastoral perspective is Roland Murphy, *Seven Books of Wisdom* (Milwaukee: Bruce, 1960). A discussion of the place of wisdom in the theology of the OT can be found in Walter Brueggemann, *In Man We Trust* (Richmond, Va.: John Knox, 1972).

The best detailed commentaries on Proverbs and Ecclesiastes are those of William McKane, *Proverbs: A New Approach* (London: SCM, 1970) and Robert Gordis, *Koheleth—The Man and His World* (New York: Schocken, 1968, first published, 1951). The Anchor Bible commentaries by R.B.Y. Scott, *Proverbs, Ecclesiastes* (Garden City: Doubleday, 1965) are useful for details of the translation and for the introduction. The best of the shorter, popular, commentaries are those in the Jerome Biblical Commentary (R.E. Brown, J. A. Fitzmyer and R.E. Murphy eds; Englewood Cliffs, N.J.: Prentice– Hall, 1968) by J. T. Forrestell (Proverbs) and R. E. Murphy (Ecclesiastes) and those in the Cambridge Bible Commentary on the New English Bible by R.N. Whybray, *The Book of Proverbs* (Cambridge: University Press, 1972) and W. J. Fuerst, *The Books of Ruth, Esther, Ecclesiastes, The Song of Songs, Lamentations* (Cambridge: University Press, 1975).